ORIGAMI ZODIAC

WESTERN AND EASTERN ZODIACS

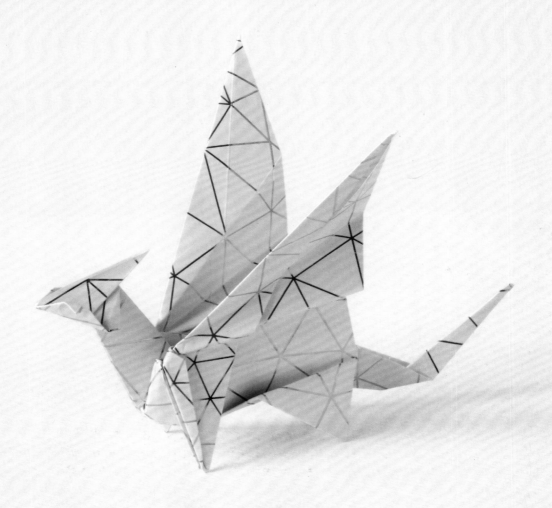

ORIGAMI ZODIAC

WESTERN AND EASTERN ZODIACS

MARK BOLITHO

jacqui
small

First published in 2018 by
Jacqui Small
An imprint of The Quarto Publishing Group
The Old Brewery
6 Blundell Street
London N7 9BH
T (0)20 7700 6700 F (0)20 7700 8066
www.QuartoKnows.com

Publisher: Jacqui Small
Commissioning and Project Editor: Joanna Copestick
Managing Editor: Emma Heyworth-Dunn
Senior Designer and Art Director: Rachel Cross
Designer: Clare Thorpe
Photography: Brent Darby
Production: Maeve Healy

ISBN: 978 1 911127 12 3

A catalogue record for this book is available
from the British Library.

2020 2019 2018
10 9 8 7 6 5 4 3 2 1

Printed in China.

Scaling and Sizes

Each project is accompanied by a scaling diagram that shows the size of the final model compared to the starting sheet of paper. The diagram is based on a square sheet with dimensions of 18 x 18cm (7 x 7in), or an equivalent rectangle. However, larger or smaller models can be made. The size of the final model can be scaled up or down by comparing the dimensions of the paper used to the sheet used in the scaling diagram.

Complexity Ratings

The projects in this book have been given a rating based on their complexity. They appear beneath the title of each project.

Easy ✳

Intermediate ✳✳

More Challenging ✳✳✳

CONTENTS

Mindful Origami 6

Getting Started 7

Yin Yang 10

WESTERN ZODIAC **12**

Aries 14

Taurus 19

Gemini 22

Cancer 26

Leo 34

Virgo 41

Libra 45

Scorpio 50

Sagittarius 56

Capricorn 62

Aquarius 66

Pisces 73

EASTERN ZODIAC **76**

Rat 78

Ox 83

Tiger 88

Rabbit 93

Dragon 98

Snake 101

Horse 104

Sheep 109

Monkey 113

Rooster 116

Dog 120

Pig 124

Resources and Acknowledgements 128

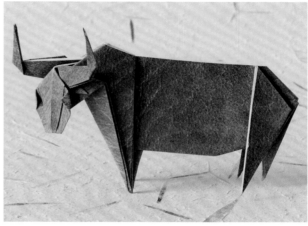

MINDFUL ORIGAMI

Welcome to the world of origami, the art of paper folding. At its heart it is the transformation of a sheet of paper into a finished model. However, it's not only a matter of creating a finished model, but also a journey of paper folding that involves creativity and contemplation along the way to produce your finished piece of work.

The word 'origami' comes from the Japanese word for paper folding. In the East the craft developed based on standard forms and traditional designs and it now has many enthusiasts around the world.

The Internet has enabled the sharing of ideas and lead to a collective enthusiasm for developing more beautiful and complex designs. In the chase for complexity, however, some of the beauty of the craft has been overlooked. This is a discrepancy I hope to redress with this book, by presenting more considered, mindfully finished works in appropriate colours and compositions.

The paper-folding process can be a meditative journey. Over time a plain sheet of paper is transformed into something wonderful. The satisfaction of origami comes not only from creating interesting designs, but also from following the folding journey and seeing your model model evolve at your fingertips. Origami offers a perfect way to explore your mindful creativity in the colours and paper choices you use, and the final composition of groups of complementary models.

The models in this collection have been selected based on the aesthetic quality of the final model and the folding processes. They are explained with step-by-step diagrams that show the sequence of folds needed for the final design.

At the start of the collection I have included instructions for a Yin Yang symbol (see page 10). This is an opportunity to gain familiarity with the diagrams and symbols used to explain the folding sequences. Some models are more complex than others and we have given a rating to each project as a guide (see page 4).

If you are new to origami, try starting with the easier models and work up to the more complex projects. I hope you enjoy folding these projects as much as I enjoyed designing them.

GETTING STARTED

Here are the basic folding techniques and symbols you'll need to complete the projects in the book.

FOLDING IN HALF

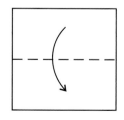

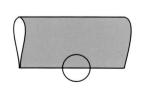

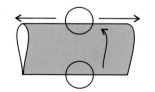

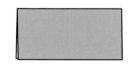

1. The step indicates that the paper should be folded in half, top to bottom.

2. First of all, line up the opposite sides of the paper and hold the edges together.

3. When the two layers are aligned, pinch the middle to hold them together. Then make the crease.

4. The paper is accurately folded in half.

ARROWS AND FOLDS

Paper-folding instructions explain the folding process with a series of steps leading to a finished model. Each step explains one or two folds in the process. Steps should be followed in order and when a step is completed, it should resemble the image shown in the next step.

The transition from one step to the next is shown by a series of lines and arrows indicating where folds should be made. The lines show where to fold and the arrows show how the paper should be moved to make folds.

Folds are described as either Mountain Folds or Valley Folds.

These names refer to how the surface will look after the fold has been completed. A Mountain Fold will fold towards the observer, forming a mountain shape, while a Valley Fold will fold away, forming a V or valley shape.They are represented by different dotted-line symbols.

ARROWS

Fold

Fold and unfold

(2) Fold over 2 layers

FOLDS	Description	In Progress	Completed
Mountain Fold			
Valley Fold			

ORIGAMI SYMBOLS

Various symbols are used to explain the folding process, such as turning the model over, rotating the model or repeating a step. The symbols on the right are the ones used in this book.

Cut

The next step will show the model turned over, top to bottom.

The next step will show the model turned over, left to right.

Repeat folds.

(5–8) Repeat steps (5 to 8).

x2 Repeat twice.

8 Unfold to step 8.

Inflate the model

Squash or sink the paper inside itself.

Viewpoint.

90° Rotate the model by 90°.

This symbol is used to highlight a reference point in the folding process.

X-ray view.

This arrow highlights layers in the paper.

DIAGRAMS

The diagrams are shown in two colours, with the coloured side being the front and the white side being the reverse. This should make the step-by-step instructions easier to follow.

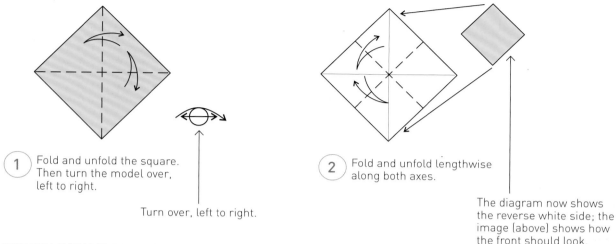

① Fold and unfold the square. Then turn the model over, left to right.

Turn over, left to right.

② Fold and unfold lengthwise along both axes.

The diagram now shows the reverse white side; the image (above) shows how the front should look.

THE FOLLOWING IS A LONGER SEQUENCE TO MAKE A PRELIMINARY BASE.

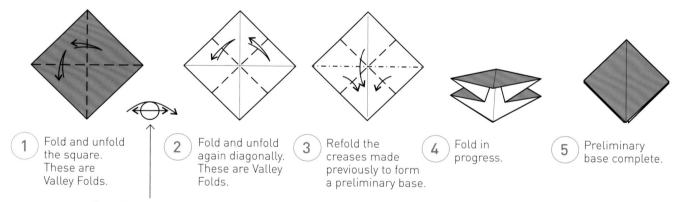

① Fold and unfold the square. These are Valley Folds.

Turn the model over.

② Fold and unfold again diagonally. These are Valley Folds.

③ Refold the creases made previously to form a preliminary base.

④ Fold in progress.

⑤ Preliminary base complete.

Origami instructions take you through a step-by-step process from start to finish. Symbols are included to explain the transition from one step to the next. Each step shows how the folded project should look and shows the folds that should be applied to progress to the next step.

When approaching a step, first check that your model resembles the step you are on. If it doesn't, unfold the last step and work back until it does. If you are happy with your model, look ahead to the next diagram to see how the model should look when the folds shown in the step you are on have been applied. Look out for reference points on the diagram to compare your model with the instructions. This should help to make sure you remain on the right track.

YIN YANG

✱✱

The Yin Yang shows how opposite forces may be complementary and work together in balance. The model works by balancing the colours from the front and reverse of the paper. Although its origins are from Chinese philosophy, the model also represents a balance between East and West.

18 X 18CM (7 X 7IN)

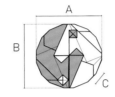

A 7cm   (2¾in)
B 7cm   (2¾in)
C 0.5cm (¼in)

START WITH A SQUARE, COLOURED SIDE UP.

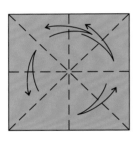

1 Fold and unfold the square in half lengthwise and diagonally along all axes.

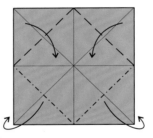

2 Fold the upper corners down to the middle and fold the lower corners to the middle, behind.

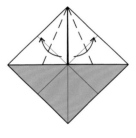

3 Fold the edges of the upper folded corners out to the folded edges.

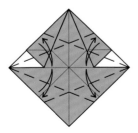

4 Fold and unfold the edges of the square to the middle creases for the upper and lower sections.

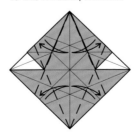

5 Fold the lower outer edges in to align them with the middle crease. Then unfold and repeat on the upper section.

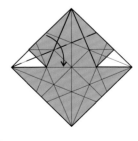

6 Fold one edge in along the crease made previously. This will cause the outer edge to touch the middle.

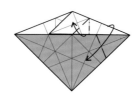

a

(7) Fold the corner over from right to left, so that the outer upper edge folds over.

(8) Fold the edge of the section up and fold the side in, along the crease made previously.

(9) (a) Fold the section up at (a) so that the lower edge folds over.

(10) Repeat the process from the previous steps and continue folding the edges in on all sides.

(11–13)

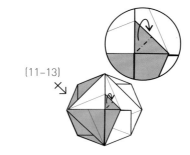

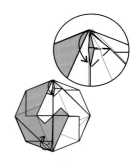

(11) Fold the corner up, separate the layers. Then squash and flatten the corner.

(12) Fold one side over.

(13) Fold the tip of the corner behind. Then repeat steps 11 to 13 on the other side. (The bubble above shows more detail).

(14) Fold the corners up, separate the layers and squash. Note, the two corners are folded differently.

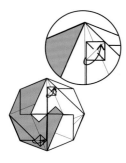

(15) Fold the upper edge over on the squashed corners to expose the colour inside.

(16) Fold the edges of the corners behind the upper layer.

(17) Fold the edges of the corners behind. This will make the model appear rounder.

(18) Complete.

Aries

✷✷

Aries the Ram is traditionally the first model in the western zodiac cycle. This project was designed from an A4 rectangle which changes the proportion and aesthetic of the final model. You can also use other international standard paper rectangles, such as letter size.

18 X 12.5CM (7 X 5IN)

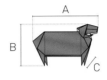

A 9cm   (3½in)
B 5cm   (2in)
C 1.5cm (⅗in)

MAKING AN 'A' RECTANGLE FROM A SQUARE.

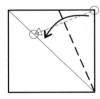

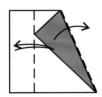

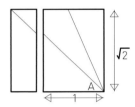

$\sqrt{2}$

1

A

① Fold the edge in diagonally to touch a crease folded along the middle of a square.

② Fold the outer edge over. The crease should touch the corner. Then unfold.

③ Cut along the crease and separate the sections.

④ The larger rectangle has the 'A' proportions 1:2 (square root).

START WITH A RECTANGLE (A4 OR LETTER), COLOURED SIDE UP.

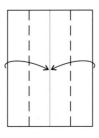

① Fold and unfold in half lengthwise. Then turn the model over, left to right.

② Fold the edges in to the middle.

③ Fold and unfold the upper corners.

④ Fold and unfold at the point where the creases touch the outer edges.

(5) Fold the upper layer down along the creases made previously on both sides.

(6) Fold the corners back up again.

(7) Turn the model over, left to right.

(8) Fold the edges of the upper section in to the middle.

(9) Fold and unfold along the edges of the folded corners.

(10) Fold the upper section down.

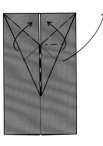

(11) Fold the corner up to the right and pinch the two sides together.

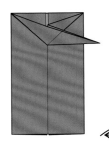

(12) Turn the model over, left to right.

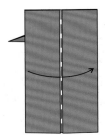

(13) Fold the upper layer over, left to right, along the middle.

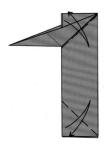

(14) Fold and unfold diagonally at either end.

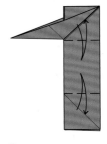

(15) Fold and unfold at the point where the diagonal fold touches the left edge.

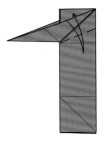

(16) Fold and unfold the upper section between the creases made previously.

17 Crimp fold the upper section into the model along the creases made previously.

18 Fold over the upper layer of the lower section and open and squash the lower section.

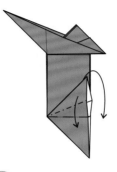

19 Fold the corner up, separate the layers and squash flat.

20 Fold the edge of the lower section back down.

21 Fold and unfold the upper and lower points diagonally along the middle.

22 Reverse fold the edges behind, along the creases made previously, to narrow the points.

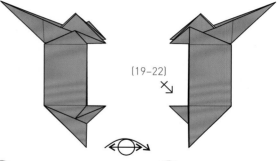

(19–22)

23 Turn the model over, left to right.

24 Repeat steps 19 to 22.

90°

25 Rotate the model by 90°.

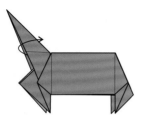

26 Open the front section slightly.

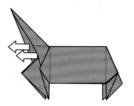

27 Fold out the paper trapped in the front section.

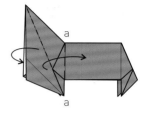

28 Fold the upper layer over along the line (a)–(a). This will open out the paper beneath.

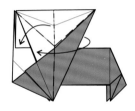

29 Fold the paper back, at the same time fold in the upper edge.

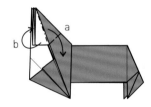

30 Fold the front layer(a) down. This will cause the edge (b) to fold in.

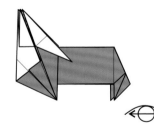

31 Turn the model over, left to right.

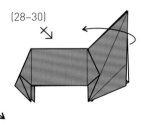

32 Repeat steps 28 to 30.

33 Hold the head and legs and crimp the upper section down.

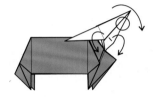

34 Tilt the head down. This shows the fold in progress.

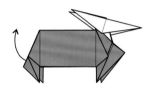

35 Fold out the trapped paper in the rear section.

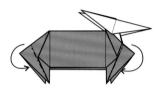

36 Reverse fold the outer corners of the lower section inside.

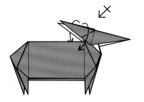

37 Fold over the corners in the upper section front and behind.

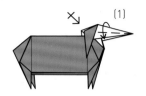

38 Fold one layer of the head over, front and behind.

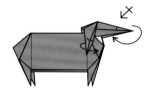

39 Reverse fold the tip of the horns front and behind. Reverse fold the tip of the head into the model.

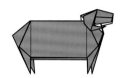

40 Complete.

Taurus

*

Taurus is designed in a similar way to Aries (see page 14). The corners become the hind legs and horns. The animal is described with clean, stylized shapes with accentuated shoulders giving a suggestion of strength.

18 X 18CM (7 X 7IN)

x 1

A 9cm (3½in)
B 7cm (2¾in)
C 2cm (¾in)

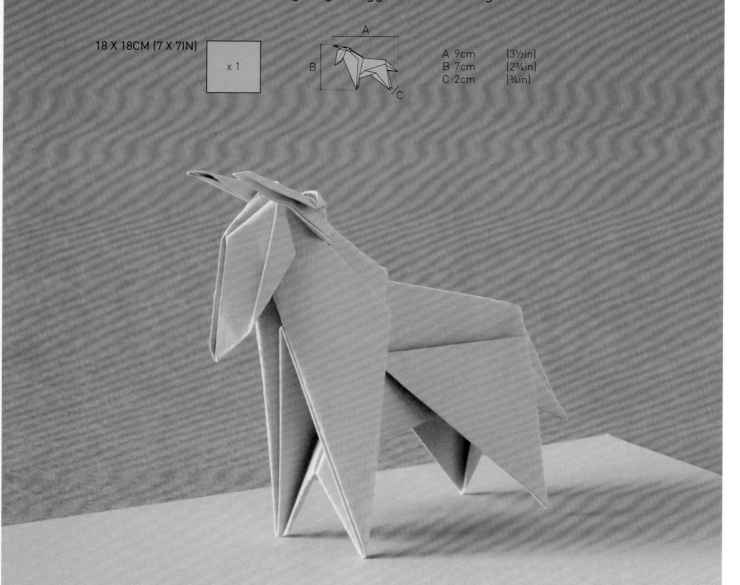

START WITH A SQUARE, COLOURED SIDE UP.

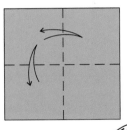

(1) Fold and unfold in half lengthwise along both axes. Then turn the model over.

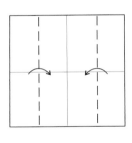

(2) Fold the outer edges in to the middle.

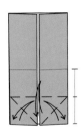

(3) Fold up the lower corners diagonally, then fold between the creases. Unfold.

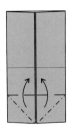

(4) Fold the upper layer of the lower sections up and squash the corners.

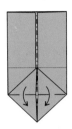

(5) Fold the corners down.

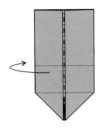

(6) Fold the model in half by folding the left side behind.

(7) Fold up the lower corner.

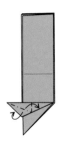

(8) Fold the point over, causing the edges to fold together.

(9) Fold the point back again.

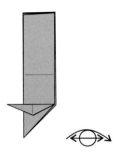

(10) Turn the model over, left to right.

(7–10)

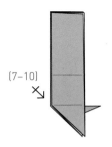

(11) Repeat steps 7 to 10.

(12) Fold the lower edges over on the front and behind.

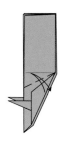

(13) Fold and unfold between the creases and the outer edge.

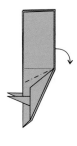

(14) Reverse fold the upper section inside, along the crease made previously.

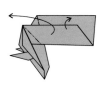

(15) Reverse fold the rear section back over, along the middle crease.

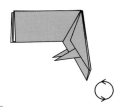

180°

(16) Rotate the model by 180°.

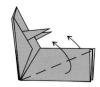

(17) Fold the corners up, front and behind.

(18) Fold the corners back down again.

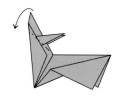

(19) Reverse fold the head into the model.

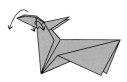

(20) Fold the edges over, front and behind, to turn the upper section inside out.

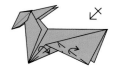

(21) Fold the edge of the section over, so the adjacent edge folds too. Repeat behind.

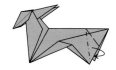

(22) Crimp fold the rear section into the model.

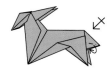

(23) Fold the lower edges of the outer section in, to narrow the tail. Repeat behind.

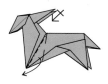

(24) Crimp fold the front section and slide the rear section into the front legs.

(25) The next steps will show a detail of the horns.

(26) Fold horns to point forwards on both sides.

(27) Fold the horns in half.

(28) Complete.

Gemini

✱✱

Gemini, or the twins, is a project that makes two human figures. Each of the figures comes from a folded waterbomb base. The corners of the square become the arms and legs, and the middle of the square becomes the head.

18 X 18CM (7 X 7IN)   x 1

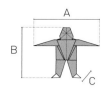

A   12cm   (4¾in)
B   11cm   (4⅓in)
C   1cm   (½in)

START WITH A SQUARE, COLOURED SIDE UP.

(1) Fold and unfold the square in half lengthwise along both axes. Then turn the paper over, left to right.

(2) Fold and unfold the square diagonally along both axes.

(3) Fold the upper edge down and, at the same time, refold the creases made previously. This is called a waterbomb base.

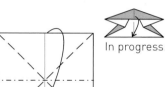

In progress.

(4) Fold and unfold the outer left corner to the middle crease. Then unfold.

(5) Fold the corner in to the crease made previously.

(6) Fold the opposite corner over to touch the corner folded in the previous step.

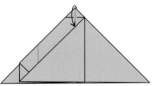

(7) Fold the top corner over to touch the adjacent folded edge.

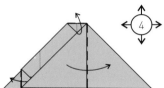

(8) Unfold back to a Waterbomb base. (Step 4).

(9) Sink the upper corner inside the model. Step 10 to 11 show an alternative method to make the fold.

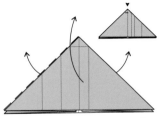

(10) Unfold back to a square.

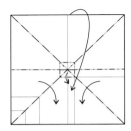

(11) Refold the waterbomb base and reverse fold the upper corner inside.

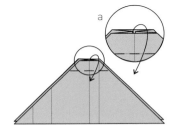

(12) Fold the upper edge down and open out the sunk point. Note the image (a) shows how the sunk point should look.

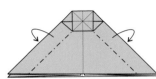

(13) Fold the edges of the front layer behind. These creases are aligned with the squashed corner.

(14) Fold and unfold the lower corners of the upper layer.

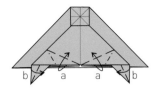

(15) Fold the edges up at (a), causing the creases made previously to fold over at (b).

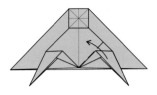

(16) Fold the arm section up along the folded edge.

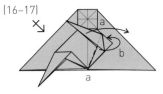

(17) Fold the arm behind, along the line (a)–(a) causing the corner (b) to fold inside the middle section and the arm to fold over. Repeat steps 16 to 17 on the other side.

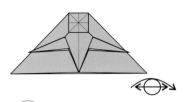

(18) Turn the model over, left to right.

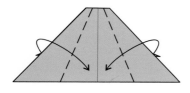

19 Fold the outer edges in to the middle crease.

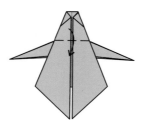

20 Fold the upper section down.

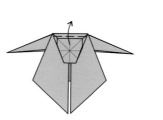

21 Fold the head back up again along the upper edge of the section.

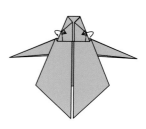

22 Fold the edges of the upper section in on both sides.

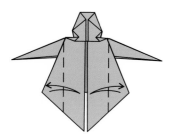

23 Fold and unfold the outer corners to the middle.

24 Reverse fold the tips of the lower corners then turn the model over left to right.

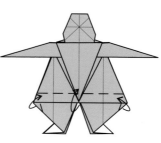

25 Fold the edge up, causing the outer corners to fold over.

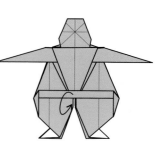

26 Fold the edge back down and into the model.

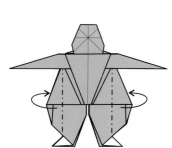

27 Fold the outer edges of the lower section behind.

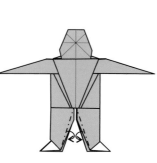

28 Fold the inner edges of the legs behind.

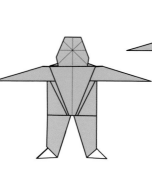

29 One person complete.

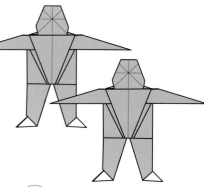

30 Make a second person to complete the twins.

Cancer

✳✳✳

Cancer, the crab, is folded from one of the classic bases in origami, the bird base.
The corners of the base are opened out to form the multiple legs of the ocean creature,
while the other two adjacent points of the base fold to become the crab's claws and eyes.

18 X 18CM (7 X 7IN)

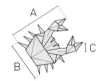

A 6.25cm   (2⅓in)
B 4.75cm   (1¾in)
C 2.5cm   (1in)

START WITH A SQUARE, COLOURED SIDE UP.

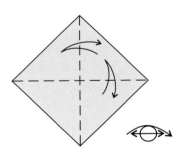

1. Fold and unfold the square in half diagonally along both axes. Then turn the paper over, left to right.

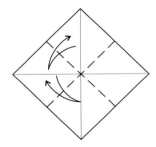

2. Fold and unfold the square in half lengthwise along both axes.

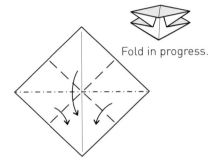

Fold in progress.

3. Fold the upper half down, at the same time refold the creases made previously, to make a preliminary base.

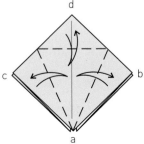

4. Fold outer edges (a–b) and (a–c) to the middle crease. Fold the upper triangle over the edges and unfold.

5. Fold the upper corner down to the crease and unfold.

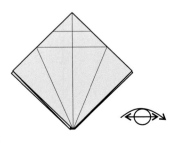

6. Turn the paper over, left to right.

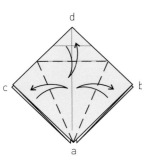

(7) Fold the outer edges (a–b) and (a–c) to the middle crease (a–d) and fold the upper triangle over the along folded edges. Unfold.

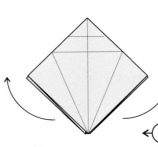

(8) The next fold will sink fold the upper corner. To do this, open the model up to a square.

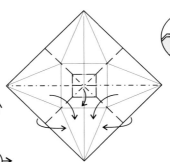

(9) Refold the preliminary base. At the same time reverse fold in the creases made in step 5 to sink the upper corner.

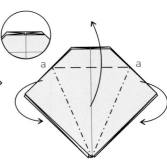

(10) Fold the upper layer up along the crease (a–a) and fold in the edges.

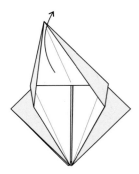

(11) Fold in progress.

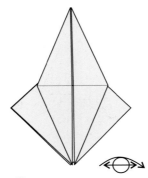

(12) Turn the model over, left to right.

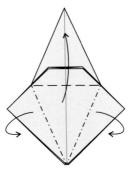

(13) Fold the upper layer up along the upper crease repeating steps (10–11). This will cause the edges to fold in.

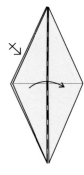

(14) Fold one side over front and behind.

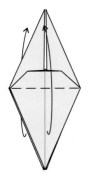

(15) Fold the points up, front and behind.

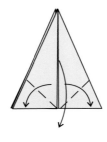

(16) Open out the paper in the upper point and fold it down.

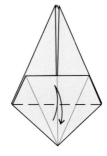

(17) Fold up and unfold the lower corner.

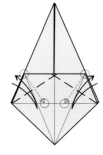

(18) Fold the corners down to touch the horizontal crease. Then unfold.

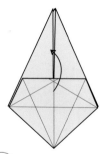

19 Unfold the upper section.

20 Fold the outer edge of the upper section to the lower edge. Then unfold.

21 Fold the upper section down and open out the layers and flatten the point.

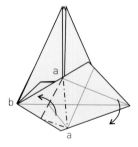

22 Fold the upper layer up to match the crease (a–a) to the edge (a–b).

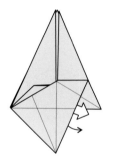

23 Fold out the paper behind the front section.

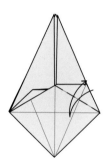

24 Fold and unfold the corner.

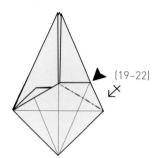

25 Sink the corner into the model, repeating steps 19 to 22.

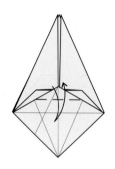

26 Fold the corner to touch the crease and unfold.

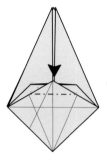

27 Sink fold the corner inside.

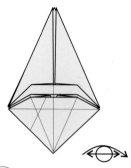

28 Turn the model over, left to right.

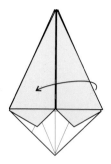

29 Fold one side over.

30 Fold the corner over; this fold will be limited by the folded paper beneath.

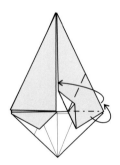

31 Fold the corner up and open out the point.

32 Fold the corner back over and fold the edge of the inner section down.

33 Fold the left side back over the right.

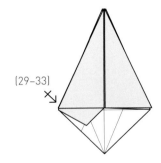

(29–33)

34 Repeat steps 29 to 33 on the other side.

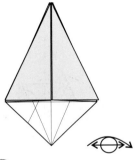

35 Turn the model over, left to right.

36 Fold the left edge down to the crease.

37 Fold the edge behind.

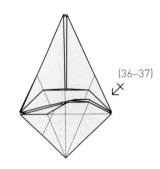

(36–37)

38 Repeat step 36 to 37 on the right side.

39 Fold the lower corner up.

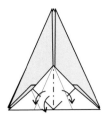

40 Fold the middle section down along diagonal folds, to make a preliminary base shape.

41 Fold the edges of the section down, making a bird base shape.

42 Pinch the points together and fold them flat to the left to lie flat.

43 Turn the model over, left to right.

44 This is the starting point for Scorpio (see page 50).

45 Fold one side over to expose a face adjacent to the folded section.

(16–42)

46 Repeat steps 16 to 42. Make sure that the legs all point in the same direction.

47 Fold one layer over, to expose an adjacent face.

48 Fold the top half of the section down.

49 Fold the tip of the point back up.

50 Fold the point in half and reverse fold the inner section to the left.

51 Turn the model over, left to right.

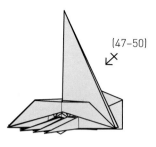

(47–50)

52 Repeat steps 47 to 50 on the other point.

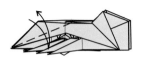

53 Fold and unfold the upper left corner in half.

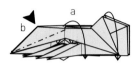

54 Open the model by folding the edge (a) down and squashing the corner (b).

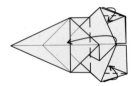

55 Fold the upper layer over. This will cause the outer edges to fold in.

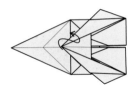

56 Tuck the corner beneath the rear section.

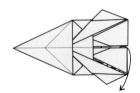

57 Reverse fold the upper edge of the section inside.

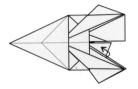

58 Slide out the folded tip (see step 49) to extend out of the model.

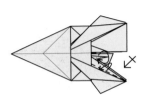

59 Fold the edge of the section in and narrow the tip. Repeat this on the lower layer.

(57–59)

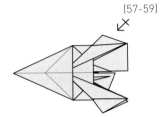

60 Repeat steps 57 to 59 on the other section.

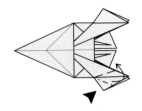

61 Fold the corner of the claw up, separate the layers and squash flat.

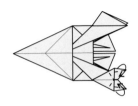

62 Fold in the edges of the claw beneath the squashed triangle.

(61–62)

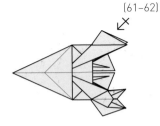

63 Repeat steps 61 to 62 on the other claw.

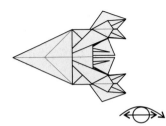

64 Turn the model over, left to right.

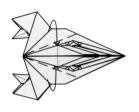

65 Fold the outer edges in and tuck them under the inner section.

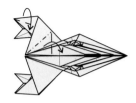

66 Fold the point back causing the adjacent edge to fold over.

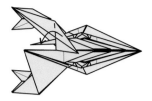

67 Fold the point back again.

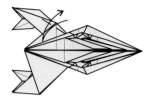

68 Fold and unfold the corner of the claw section.

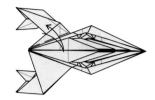

69 Fold and unfold along the adjacent folded edge.

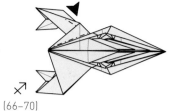

(66–70)

70 Sink the edge of the corner inside along the creases made previously. Then repeat steps 66 to 70 on the other claw.

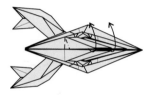

71 Fold out two legs by holding the points and sliding them forward .Then flatten them to hold them in place.

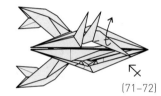

(71–72)

72 Fold out the final leg and repeat the process on the other side (steps 71 to 72).

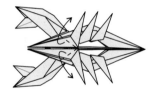

73 Fold over the front legs on both sides.

74 Fold the corner over and tuck it under the front section.

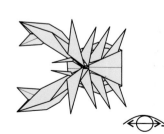

75 Turn the model over, left to right.

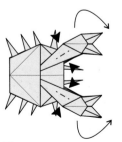

76 Pinch the forward sections together to narrow and shape the claws.

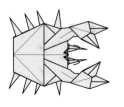

77 Fold the two anenna up.

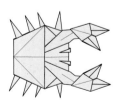

78 Cancer the crab is complete.

Leo

***

Leo is another detailed project. The lion is presented face on in a graphical style, eyes looking out from beneath a heavy brow. The model explores using folds to make textures and the mane is made from a series of crimp folds around the lion's face.

18 X 18CM (7 X 7IN)

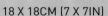

x1

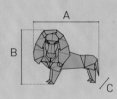

A 7.5cm   (3in)
B 6.75cm   (2½in)
C 2.25cm   (¾in)

START WITH A SQUARE, COLOURED SIDE UP.

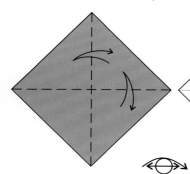

1 Fold and unfold the square in half diagonally along both axes. Turn the paper over, left to right.

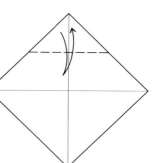

2 Fold and unfold the upper corner to the middle of the square.

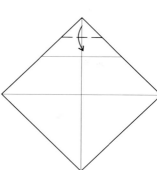

3 Fold the upper corner down to touch the adjacent crease.

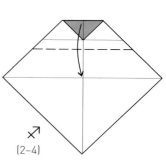

(2–4)

4 Fold the upper edge down to touch the middle crease. Then Repeat steps 2 to 4 on the lower section.

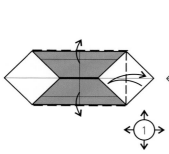

5 Fold and unfold the outer corner in. Then unfold the model back to a square.

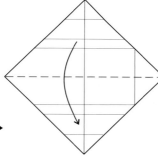

6 Fold the paper in half diagonally.

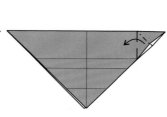

7 Fold over the right corner, separate the layers and squash the point flat.

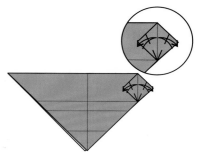

8 Fold and unfold both edges of the section in to the middle crease.

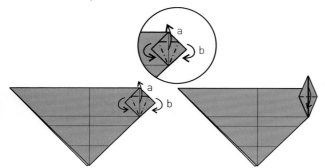

9 Fold the upper layer up at (a) between the creases. This will cause the edges (b) to fold in.

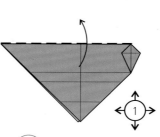

10 Fold the corner back down.

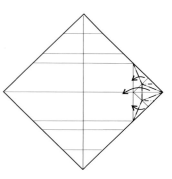

11 Open the model up back to a square.

12 Fold in the right corner along the creases made previously.

LEO 35

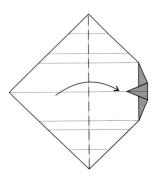

(13) Fold the left corner over along the middle crease.

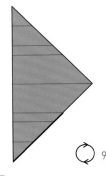

(14) Rotate the model 90° clockwise.

90°

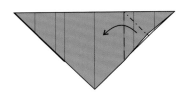

(15) Fold the right corner in to be perpendicular to the base, separate the layers and squash the point flat.

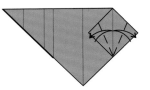

(16) Fold and unfold both edges to the middle crease.

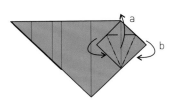

(17) Fold the upper layer up at (a) between the creases. This will cause the edges (b) to fold in.

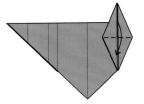

(18) Fold the point down again.

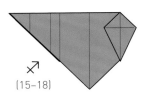

(15–18)

(19) Repeat steps 15 to 18 on the other side.

(20) Open the paper and unfold the two outer folded sections.

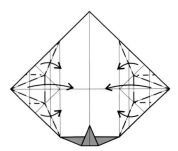

(21) Refold the corners in to the model along the creases made previously.

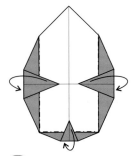

(22) Fold the three folded outer sections behind.

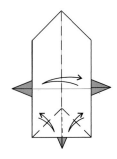

(23) Fold the model in half and fold the lower edge into the model. Then unfold.

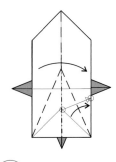

(24) Fold the model in half and reverse fold the inner section. This will make the crease made in step 23 touch the outer edge.

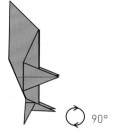

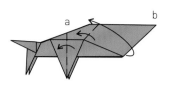

25 Reverse fold the segment back into the model.

26 Fold the rear section forward by making two crimp folds on either side and sliding the section forward.

27 Rotate the model by 90° clockwise.

28 Fold the front layer over at (a), this will cause the outer section (b) to fold up.

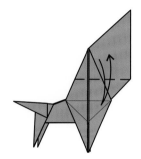

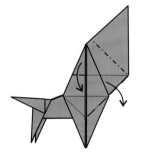

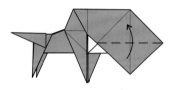

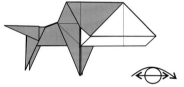

29 Fold and unfold the upper section.

30 Fold down the top section and open it out.

31 Fold the lower corner up.

32 Turn the model over, left to right.

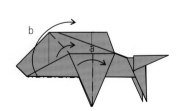

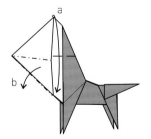

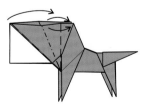

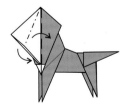

33 Fold the point (a) over This will cause the outer section (b) to fold up.

34 Fold the upper point (a) down and reverse fold out the middle section (b).

35 Fold the front section in by making two crimp folds on either side to slide the front into the middle.

36 Fold the front corner up, separate the layers and squash it flat.

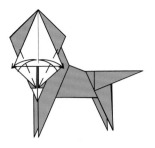

37 Fold and unfold the edges to the middle crease.

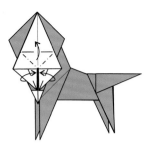

38 Fold the edge up, this will cause the lower sides to fold in.

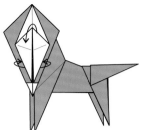

39 Unfold the paper trapped behind. Then refold, making a bird base shape.

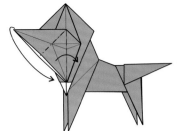

40 Fold the corner up, separate the layers and squash it flat.

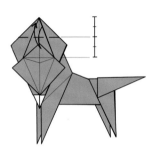

41 Fold the upper corner down to the adjacent crease. Unfold.

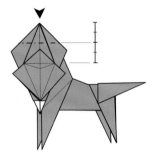

42 Sink fold the upper corner into the model.

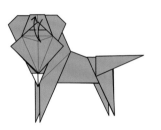

43 Fold and unfold the corner down to the adjacent crease.

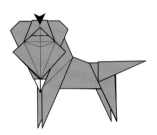

44 Sink fold the corner inside the model.

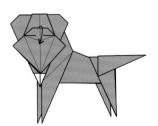

45 Fold the edge down and open out the middle section.

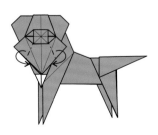

46 Fold the edges of the section behind.

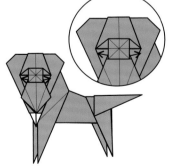

47 Fold out the paper beneath to form the eyes.

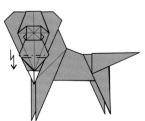

48 Fold the lower section up and into the model then down again, for a zigzag fold.

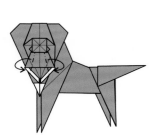

49 Fold the edges of the section behind.

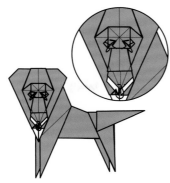

50 Fold up the edges of the eyes to round them. Then fold in the tip of the nose.

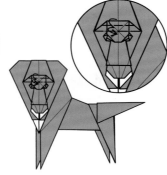

51 Fold the upper edge down and then over again to form the brow.

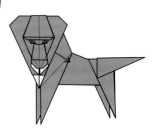

52 Reverse fold out the upper right side of the head.

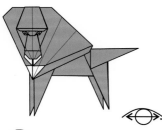

53 Turn the model over, left to right.

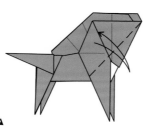

54 Fold and unfold where indictated.

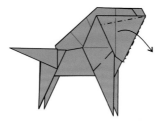

55 Fold the section out and open it flat.

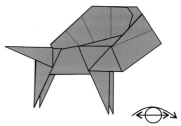

56 Turn the model over, left to right.

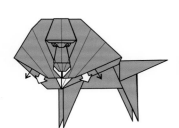

57 Reverse fold out the trapped paper in the lower part of this section.

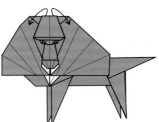

58 Reverse fold the upper corners of the mane behind the head.

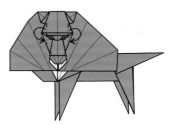

59 Fold the outer corners of the head behind.

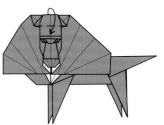

60 Fold the upper edge over.

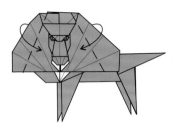

61 Fold the edges of the mane over.

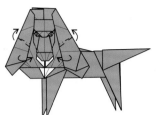

62 Fold the sides of the mane in by making crimp folds part way up on both sides to shape the head.

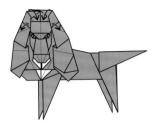

63 Make further crimp folds in the upper layer to continue shaping the mane over the head.

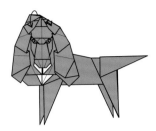

64 Fold the upper corner over.

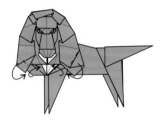

65 Reverse fold the lower corners into the mane.

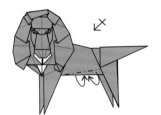

66 Fold the lower edges into the model to narrow the body on both sides.

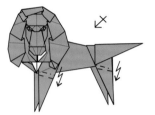

67 Fold the legs into and out of the model, making zigzag crimp folds. Repeat behind.

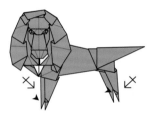

68 Reverse fold the points and fold them back again to make feet (see step 69).

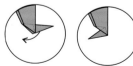

69 Foot folds in progress. Repeat this on all points to make feet.

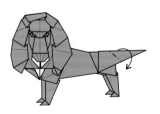

70 Reverse fold the tail.

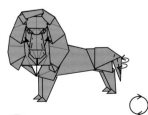

71 Fold the edges of the tail inside. Pinch the nose to narrow it then tilt the model slightly to stand.

72 Complete.

Virgo
**

Virgo, is made from half a blinzed frog base and also explores different folding styles. The linear angular upper section is complimented by the lower rounded more fluid skirt.

18 X 18CM (7 X 7IN)

x1

A 8.5cm   (3⅓in)
B 12.5cm   (5in)
C 3.5cm   (1⅓in)

START WITH A SQUARE, COLOURED SIDE UP.

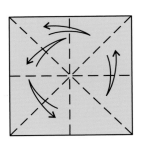

1 Fold and unfold the square lengthwise and diagonally along both axes.

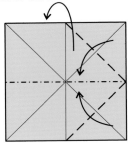

2 Fold the corners to the middle. Then fold the model in half behind.

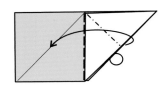

3 Fold the point to be perpendicular to the base, separate the layers and squash the point.

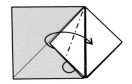

4 Raise and squash the corner.

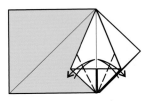

5 Fold and unfold the edges to the middle crease.

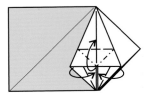

6 Fold the edge up, this will cause the lower edges to fold in on both sides, making a petal fold.

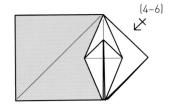

7 Repeat steps 4 to 6 on the adjacent triangle behind.

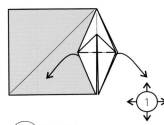

8 Fold the corners down and open out back to a square, coloured side down.

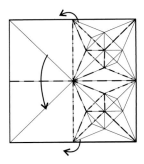

9 Refold the folds where indicated. This will create half a blinzed frog base.

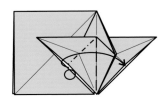

10 Raise and squash the point.

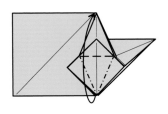

11 Fold the squashed point up to make a bird base shape.

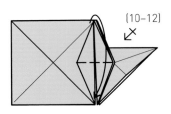

12 Fold the corner down. Then repeat steps 10 to 12 behind.

42 WESTERN ZODIAC

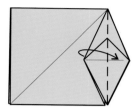

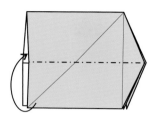

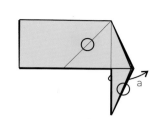

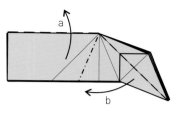

(13) Fold both layers of the edges over, left to right, in front and behind.

(14) Fold the upper layer behind and into the model. Repeat behind.

(15) Hold the model where indicated by the "Os" and slide the points (a) upwards.

(16) Fold the lower edge up at (a). At the same time, open up the point (b) and fold it over.

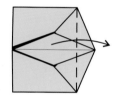

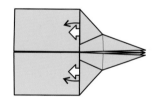

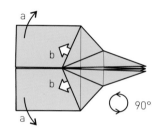

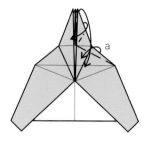

(17) Make sure the layers in the point are evenly distributed. Then Fold the section back again.

(18) Reverse fold out the triangular points trapped inside.

(19) (a) Slide out the upper layer, causing the paper at (b) to fold out. Then rotate the model by 90°.

(20) Fold the edge over at (a). This will cause the point above to fold down. Open the point and squash it flat.

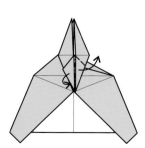

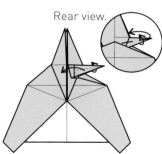

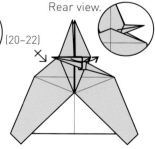

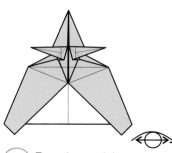

(21) Fold the point up to the right.

(22) Fold the point over to the left, causing the edge behind to fold up and narrow.

(23) Fold the point back again. Repeat steps 20 to 22 on the other side.

(24) Turn the model over, left to right.

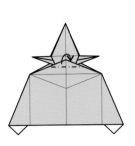

25) Fold the corner behind and into the model.

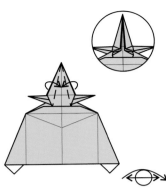

26) Fold both layers of the edges of the upper section in to the middle. Then turn the model over, left to right.

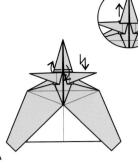

27) Fold the upper point down and up again, making a zigzag fold. Then unfold.

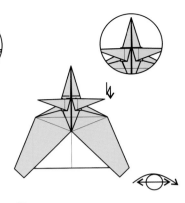

28) Reverse fold the point into itself by opening the point and folding it in and out. Then turn the model over.

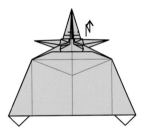

29) Fold the upper section down and up again making a zigzag fold.

30) Open out the layers in the folded point to shape the head.

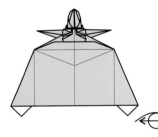

31) Turn the model over, left to right.

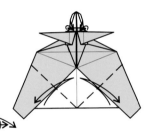

32) Fold the upper corners in to shape the neck. Then fold and unfold the lower corners as shown.

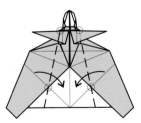

33) Fold one side over. Note the intersection of the creases. Then fold in the other side.

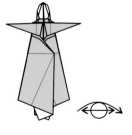

34) Turn the model over, left to right.

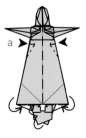

35) Fold the lower section over twice and into the base. Then push in the sides to shape the body.

36) Complete.

Libra

**

Libra represents balance. The model is made from one of the classic origami bases, the bird base. Two of the opposing points fold out to form the arms, with the tips opening out to form the weighing pans.

18 X 18CM (7 X 7IN)   x 1

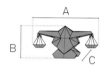

A 11.5cm   (4½in)
B 5.5cm   (2in)
C 2cm   (¾in)

THE MODEL STARTS WITH A BIRD BASE, WITH THE UPPER CORNER REVERSED INSIDE.
(FOLLOW CANCER STEPS 1 TO 14, (PAGES 26 TO 28).

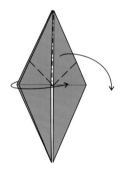

(1) Fold the edge over and reverse fold the point to the right.

(2) Turn the model over, left to right.

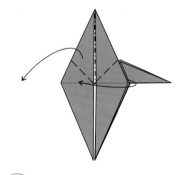

(3) Fold the side back, at the same time reverse fold the point down to the left.

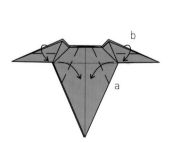

(4) Fold the edges to the centre crease (a) and the top edge over (b), on both sides.

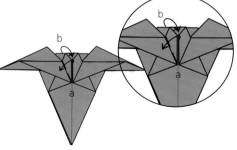

(5) Fold the edge of the trapped layer over (a). This will cause a second fold at (b).

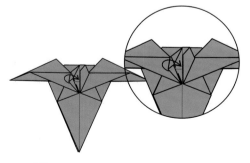

(6) Fold the edge back over.

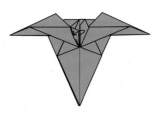

7 Fold the edge back over and tuck it into the adjacent pocket.

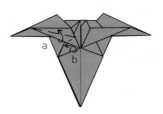

8 Fold the edge up at (a). This will cause the lower section to fold over at (b).

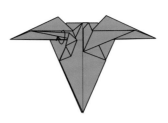

9 Fold the edge down and behind, into the model.

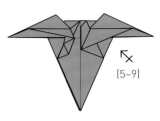

(5–9)

10 Repeat steps 5 to 9 on the other side.

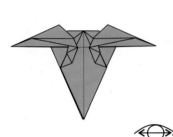

11 Turn the model over, left to right.

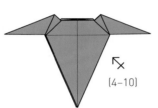

(4–10)

12 Repeat steps 4 to 10.

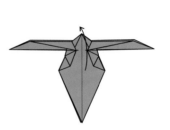

13 Fold the top layer of the lower section up.

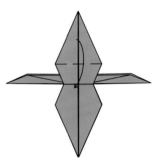

14 Fold the point down again.

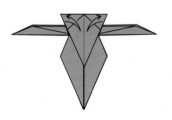

15 Fold and unfold the outer corners to the middle crease.

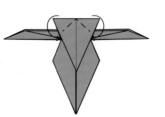

16 Reverse fold the corners into the model.

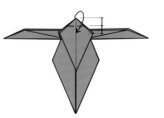

17 Fold the top point over.

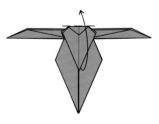

18 Fold the point up along the folded edge made in the previous step. Then flatten.

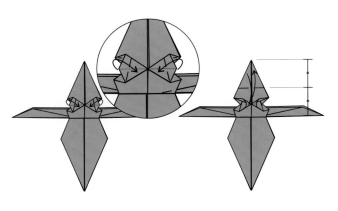 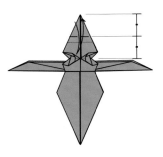 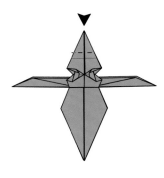

19) Fold the outer edges in and fold over the adjacent edges.

20) Fold and unfold the top point where indicated.

21) Fold and unfold between the tip and the top of the folded section.

22) Sink fold the tip into the model along the crease made in the previous step. This turns the point inside out.

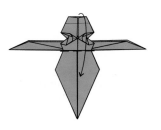 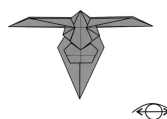 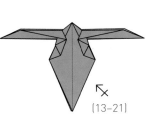 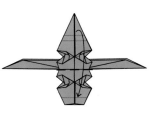

23) Fold the top layer down again.

24) Turn the model over, left to right.

25) Repeat steps 13 to 21 to fold the point without sinking the tip inside.

26) Fold the top section down.

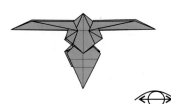 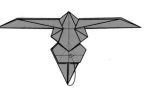 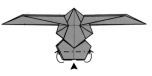 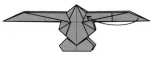

27) Turn the model over, left to right.

28) Fold the lower point up and into the pocket in the upper layer

29) Reverse fold the lower edge into the model along the creases made previously.

30) Fold the right side in causing the tip to touch the middle crease.

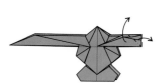

31 Fold the point up, perpendicular to the model. Open the layers and flatten.

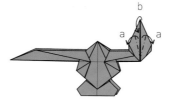

32 Fold out the edges at (a). This will cause the tip to fold over (b).

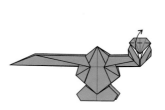

33 Fold the corner back up.

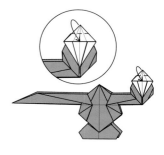

34 Fold the top of the corner over.

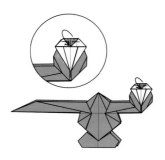

35 Fold the top edge over again.

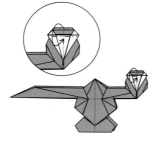

36 Fold the top edge over and tuck it behind into the pocket beneath.

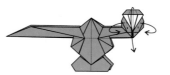

37 Fold the section down where indicated. This will cause the outer edges to fold in.

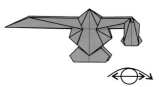

38 Turn the model over, left to right.

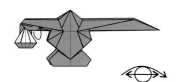

39 Fold the edge up and into the pocket above. Then turn the model over.

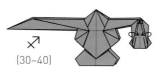

40 Fold the two edges in. Then repeat steps 30 to 40 on the other side.

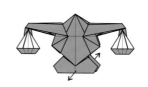

41 Open the base slightly to enable the model to stand.

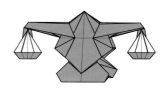

42 Complete.

Scorpio

**

Scorpio uses similar folding sequences to Cancer. Both models start from a birdbase. However, for Scorpio the opposite points are opened to form the legs, while the points on the other axes are folded to make a texture for the back and the tail of the scorpion.

18 X 18CM (7 X 7IN)

x1

A 7cm   (2¾in)
B 4.75cm   (1¾in)
C 5cm   (2in)

START WITH A SQUARE, COLOURED SIDE UP.
THEN FOLLOW THE STEPS FOR CANCER UNTIL STEP 43 (PAGES 26 TO 31).

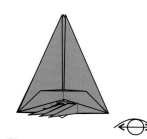

(1) Turn the model over, left to right.

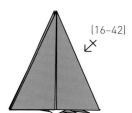

(16-42)

(2) Repeat steps 16 to 42 of Cancer (see page 26 to 30). Ensure the legs front and behind face the same way.

(3) Fold one side over.

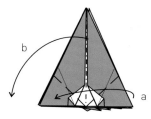

(4) Fold the open section (a) back together and reverse fold the point (b) down.

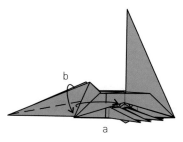

(5) Fold the point over at (a) and fold the upper edge (b) down.

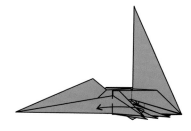

(6) Fold the section back to the left.

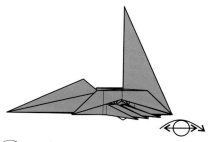

(7) Turn the model over, left to right.

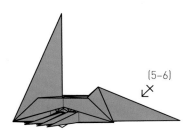

(5-6)

(8) Repeat steps 5 to 6.

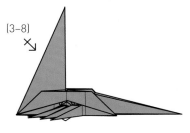

(3-8)

(9) Repeat steps 3 to 8 on the other point.

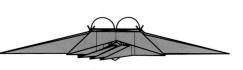

(10) Fold down the inner corners inside the model.

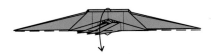

11 Fold the front layer down.

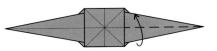

12 Fold one side up beneath the middle squashed square.

13 Fold and unfold the inner corner.

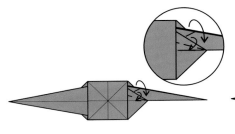

14 Fold the front edge over and fold the layer behind, making a triangular fold.

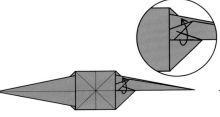

15 Unfold the previous step.

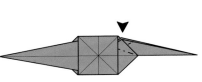

16 Sink fold the corner into the model. This turns the corner inside out.

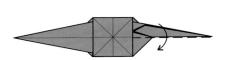

17 Fold the upper edge down.

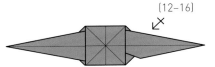

18 Repeat steps 12 to 16 on the upper section.

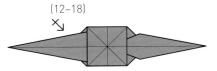

19 Repeat steps 12 to 18 on the other side.

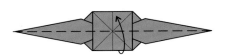

20 Fold the lower section back up.

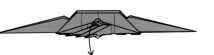

21 Fold the leg section down.

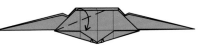

22 Fold the corner down to the adjacent crease.

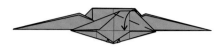

23 Fold the opposite corner over.

24 Fold the outer corners of both the triangles in.

25 Fold the lower section up.

26 Turn the model over, left to right.

(21–25)

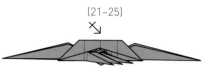

27 Repeat steps 21 to 25.

28 Fold one side down and open the model.

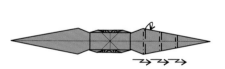

29 Fold the right point in and out again, making a series of zigzag folds to add texture to the tail.

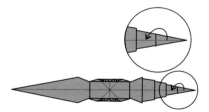

30 Fold the tip of the point over.

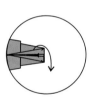

31 Pinch the folded point and fold it down.

32 Fold out the trapped paper.

33 Reverse fold the tip to the right and then back to make a bird's foot fold.

34 The sting is complete.

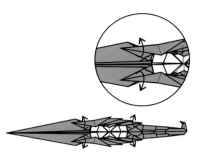

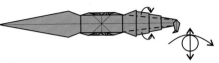

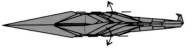

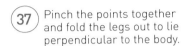

(35) Fold the outer edges behind to narrow the tail. Then turn the model over, top to bottom.

(36) Fold out the edges to be perpendicular to the base.

(37) Pinch the points together and fold the legs out to lie perpendicular to the body.

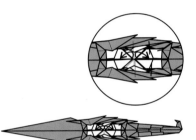

(38) Fold the inner corners out to make a 3-D inner section.

(39) Turn the model over, top to bottom.

(40) Fold the left point over along the adjacent edge of the middle section.

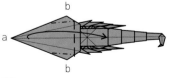

(41) Pinch the points together.

(42) Open out the folded-back section and fold over.

(43) Fold the section (a) back again along a new crease and fold the edges (b) in.

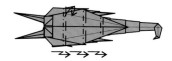

(44) Fold the section back and out again, making a series of zigzag folds.

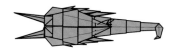

(45) Fold the outer corner behind and tuck it into the pocket formed by the paper in the layer beneath.

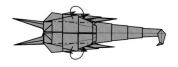

(46) Fold the sides in and tuck them into the pockets behind.

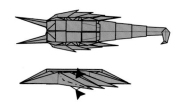

(47) Pinch a leg and fold it out.

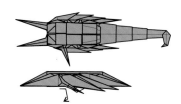

(48) Bend the leg down and fold over the tip to make a foot.

(47–48) x 7

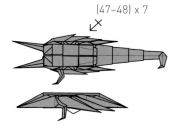

(49) Repeat steps 47 to 48 on the other leg points.

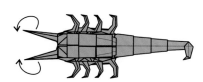

(50) Pinch the front points and bend them.

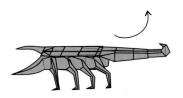

(51) Curl and shape the tail.

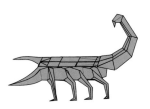

(52) Complete.

Sagittarius
✷✷

Sagittarius is a Centaur – half man, half horse. The model starts with a blinzed frog base.
This base has eight points that evolve into the four legs and tail of the horse combined
with the two arms and head of a man.

18 X 18CM (7 X 7IN)

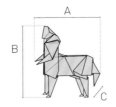

A 6.25cm   (2⅓in)
B 7cm   (2¾in)
C 1.5cm   (¾in)

START WITH A SQUARE, COLOURED SIDE UP.

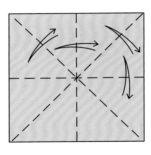

(1) Fold and unfold lengthwise and
diagonally along both axes.

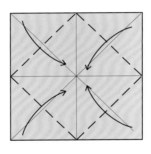

(2) Fold all the corners into
the middle.

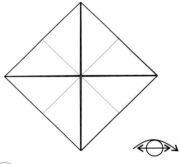

(3) Turn the model over,
left to right.

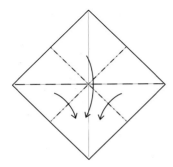

(4) Fold the upper section down
and reverse fold the sides in,
making a preliminary base.

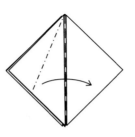

(5) Fold the point up to be
perpendicular to the base,
separate the layers and
squash flat.

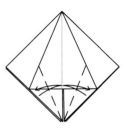

(6) Fold and unfold the lower
edges to the middle crease.

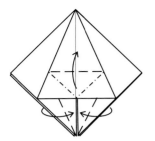

(7) Fold the edge up along the middle, this will cause the edges to fold in.

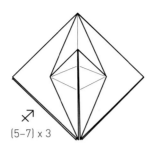

(5–7) x 3

(8) Repeat steps 5 to 7 on the other three sides.

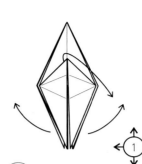

1

(9) Open the model out back to a square.

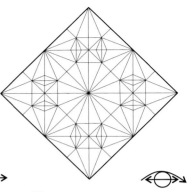

(10) Turn the model over, left to right.

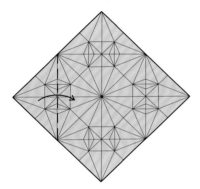

(11) Fold the left corner in to the middle.

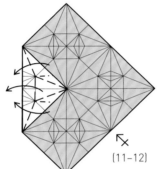

(11–12)

(12) Fold the point out again and refold the creases made previously. Repeat steps 11 to 12 on the other side.

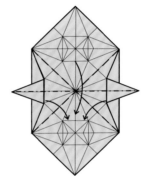

(13) Fold the upper section over and, at the same time, reverse fold the sides in.

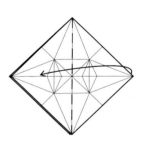

(14) Fold one side over front and behind.

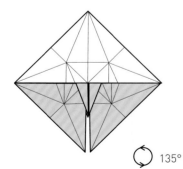

135°

(15) Rotate the model by 135°.

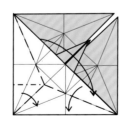

(16) Fold upper layer of upper left corner down and reverse fold inner section.

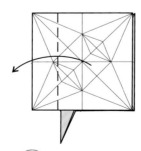

(17) Fold the edge to the left.

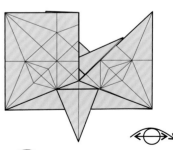

(18) Turn the model over, left to right.

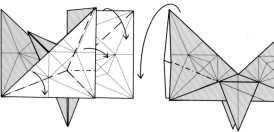

19 Fold the edges of the front section down along the creases made previously.

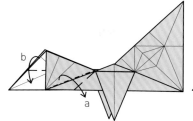

20 Reverse fold the upper left point inside.

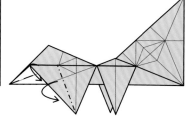

21 Fold the corner over and down at (a) and fold over the layer behind at (b).

22 Fold the edge behind. This will make the adjacent edge fold over and narrow the point.

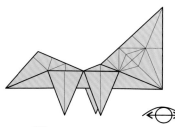

23 Turn the model over, left to right.

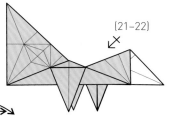

(21-22)

24 Repeat steps 21 to 22.

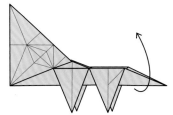

25 Reverse the right point up.

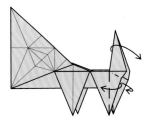

26 Fold the edges over on both sides and fold the point down.

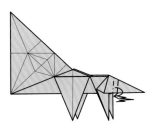

27 Fold the point in to one of the legs, then reverse it out again.

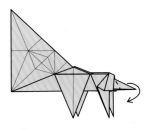

28 Reverse fold the point to shape the tail.

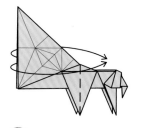

29 Fold the outer layers over front and behind to turn point inside-out.

This is the starting point for Capricorn.

30 Reverse the point in, to one side of the central section.

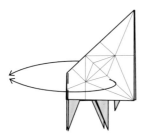

31 Fold the outer layers around and turn them right side out again.

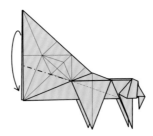

32 Reverse fold the point inside the front section.

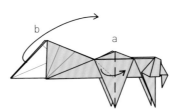

33 Folding the upper layer over at (a), causing section (b) to open up.

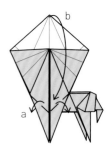

34 Fold the sides out at (a), opening the point (b) and folding it down.

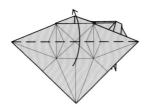

35 Fold the corner up.

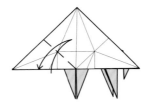

36 Fold the corner up and unfold.

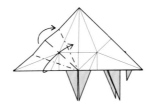

37 Fold the corner back up and, at the same time, reverse fold the inner section inside.

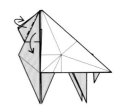

38 Fold the upper point down and fold the left edge behind.

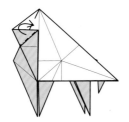

39 Fold the upper left corner behind and into the model.

40 Reverse fold the point inside.

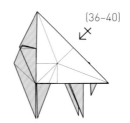

41 Repeat steps 36 to 40 on the other side.

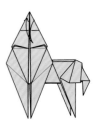

42 Fold the upper point down to the crease, and unfold.

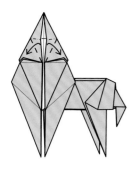

(43) Fold the upper point down and open it out.

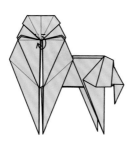

(44) Fold the tip behind.

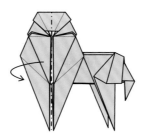

(45) Fold the left edge of the front section behind.

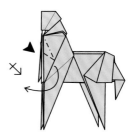

(46) Reverse fold the points in and back out again to form the arms.

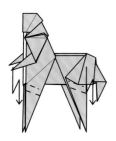

(47) Reverse fold the legs in and out of the model making zigzag folds. Repeat behind.

(48) Hold the head section and slide it up slightly.

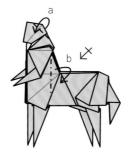

(49) Fold the upper edge over at (a). Then fold the edge (b) into the model Repeat behind.

(50) The next steps will show a detail of the feet.

(51) Reverse fold the tip of the leg back and then forwards to make a foot.

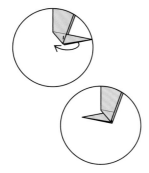

(52) Detail of the foot-folding process.

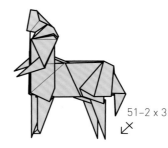

51–2 x 3

(53) Repeat steps 51 to 52 on the other three legs.

(54) Complete. Fold over the corner inside

Capricorn

**

Capricorn, the goat, is made in a similar way to Sagittarius. Both models have a similar lower section. However, for this model, the upper section folds up to become the head and horns of the creature.

18 X 18CM (7 X 7IN)

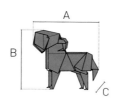

A 7.25cm (2¾in)
B 6.25cm (2⅓in)
C 3.25cm (1⅓in)

START BY COMPLETING STEPS 1 TO 30 OF SAGITTARIUS (PAGES 56 TO 59).
THEN TURN THE MODEL OVER, LEFT TO RIGHT.

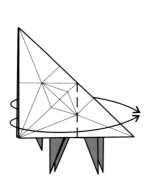

1. Fold the outer layers over turning the section inside out.

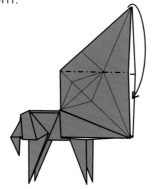

2. Reverse fold the upper corner into the model.

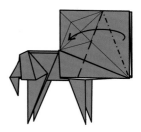

3. Fold upper edge to the left so the outer edge folds over.

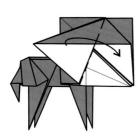

4. Fold the point back.

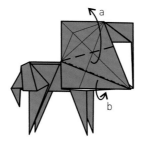

5. Fold the point (a) up and fold the lower layer (b) in.

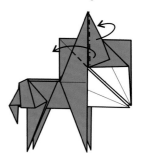

6. Swivel the upper point to the left and fold it in half.

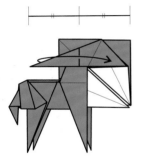

7) Fold the point over to touch the opposite edge. This will cause the layer behind to fold in half.

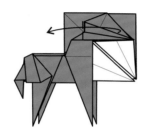

8) Fold the point back again. Keep the edge folded over from step 7.

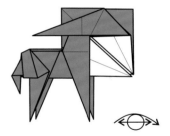

9) Turn the model over, left to right.

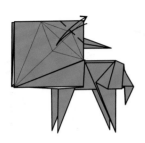

10) Fold and unfold the upper right corner.

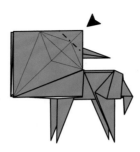

11) Open sink the corner inside the model. This will turn the corner inside out.

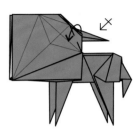

12) Fold over the edge of the sunk corner. Repeat behind.

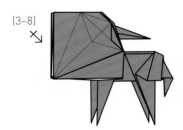

13) Repeat steps 3 to 8.

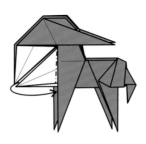

14) Reverse fold the lower corner over and into the model.

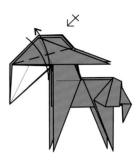

15) Fold and unfold the upper edge of the head diagonally. Repeat behind.

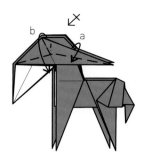

16 Fold (b) the top of the head over and (a) narrow the adjacent point. Repeat behind.

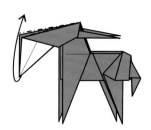

17 Reverse fold the lower point up.

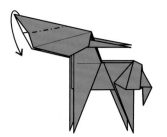

18 Reverse fold the upper left tip inside the model.

19 Fold the edges of the point inside. Repeat behind.

20 Fold the tip back up again.

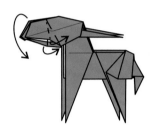

21 Crimp fold the head on both sides and tilt it downwards.

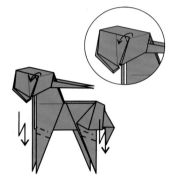

22 Fold the tip of the corner over to make an eye. Then fold the points in and out to shape the legs. Repeat behind.

23 Reverse fold the horns to shape them.

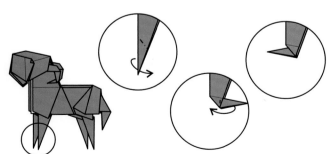

24 Reverse fold the tips of the leg.

25 Then fold the point back again to complete the bird's foot procedure.

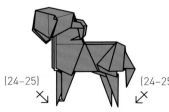

(24–25)

26 Repeat the foot folding on the other three legs.

27 Complete.

Aquarius
✳✳✳

Aquarius is represented as a water carrier. This stylized model shows water being poured from a container balanced on the shoulder of a kneeling figure. Different folding techniques are applied to make textures of the model and the falling water.

18 X 18CM (7 X 7IN) x 1

A 4.5cm   (1¾in)
B 7.75cm   (3in)
C 2.25cm   (¾in)

START WITH A SQUARE, COLOURED SIDE UP.

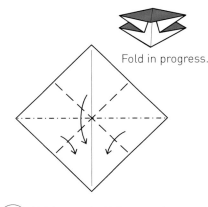

Fold in progress.

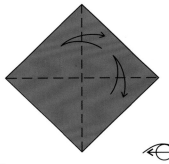

1) Fold and unfold the square in half diagonally along both axes. Then turn the paper over, left to right.

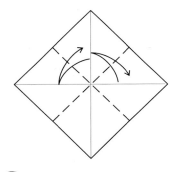

2) Fold and unfold the square lengthwise along both axes.

3) Fold upper half down and simultaneously refold the creases made previously to make a preliminary base.

4) Fold the whole model in half, then unfold.

5) Fold the upper corner down to the crease and unfold.

6) Sink fold the upper corner into the model.

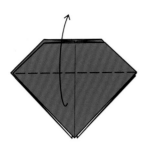

7 Fold the top layer only up.

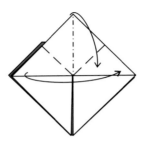

8 Fold one layer to the right and reverse fold the middle section.

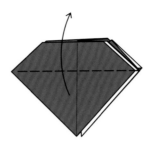

9 Fold the corner up.

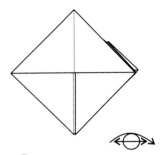

10 Turn the model over, left to right.

11 Fold the upper layer over, left to right.

12 Fold the upper layer of the lower corner up.

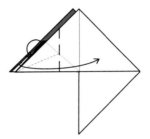

13 Fold the left corner over and open and squash the layer behind.

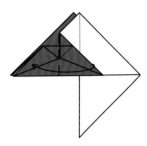

14 Fold the corner back again.

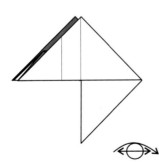

15 Turn the model over, left to right.

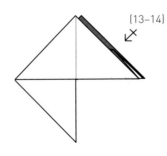

(13–14)

16 Repeat steps 13 to 14.

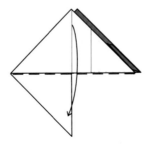

17 Fold the upper corner of the upper layer down.

18 Reverse fold the inner corners caused by the sink fold.

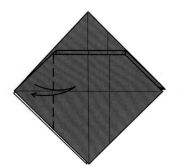

19 Fold and unfold one side over to the middle.

20 Fold the lower section up, this will cause the adjacent side to fold in.

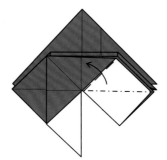

21 Fold the corner up and open up the paper in the layer beneath.

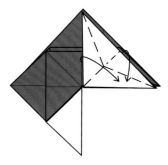

22 Fold the corner down and reverse fold the inner section inside.

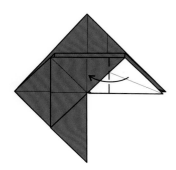

23 Fold the corner to the left and squash the paper in the layer below.

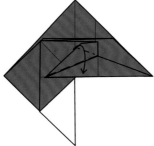

24 Fold the edge over and squash the paper above.

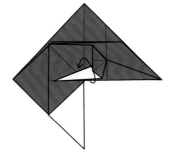

25 Fold the upper layer behind, turning the point inside out.

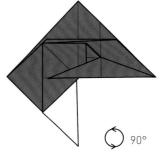

90°

26 Rotate the model by 90°.

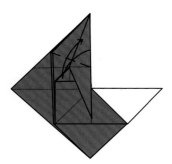

27 Fold and unfold the upper section.

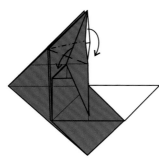

28 Fold down the upper section along the crease made previously, separate the layers and squash flat.

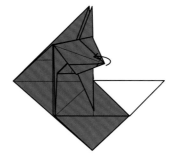

29 Fold the corner over.

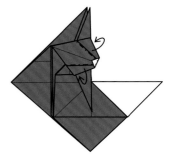

30 Fold the edges of the middle section behind.

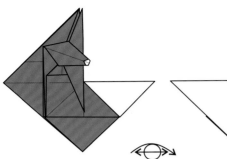

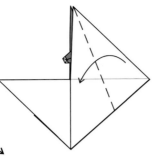

31 Turn the model over, left to right.

32 Fold the upper layer of the right corner over.

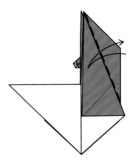

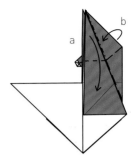

33 Fold the upper edge over and then unfold.

34 Fold the point (a) down and fold the edge (b) back over.

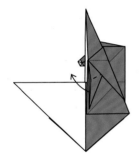

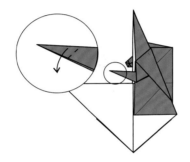

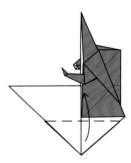

35 Reverse fold the point.

36 Reverse fold the point down, making a bird's foot.

37 Fold the point back up again to complete the hand.

38 Fold the lower corner up.

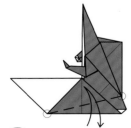

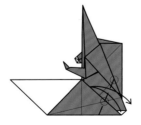

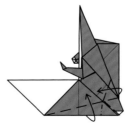

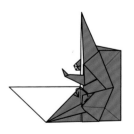

39 Fold and unfold the lower edge through all the layers.

40 Fold and unfold the lower corner. Ensure the fold is aligned with the reference points.

41 Fold the two edges in together along the creases made previously.

42 Fold the corner behind.

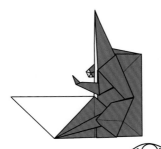

43 Turn the model over, left to right.

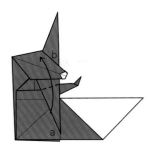

44 Fold the point up. Ensure the tip (a) is above the edge (b).

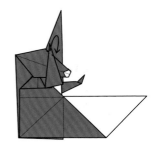

45 Fold the tip of the point behind and between the layers in the edge behind.

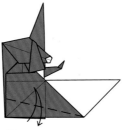

46 Fold and unfold the lower edge diagonally. This fold should align with the folded edge behind.

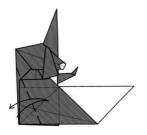

47 Fold and unfold the lower left corner. This fold should align with the folded edge behind.

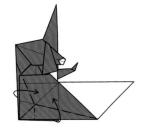

48 Fold the lower section up and refold the creases made in the previous steps.

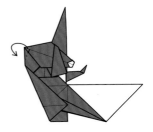

49 Fold the upper left corner behind.

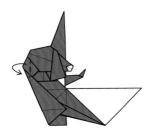

50 Fold the left edge behind to shape the figure.

51 Fold the section to be perpendicular to the base. Separate and squash the point.

52 Fold and unfold the lower edges to the middle.

53 Fold the upper layer upwards and fold the sides in.

54 Fold one side over.

55 Reverse fold the section inside.

56 Turn the model over, left to right.

57 Fold and unfold the upper section.

58 Reverse fold the upper point inside itself.

59 Fold one edge over to open the point.

60 Fold the edges over and turn them inside out. Open out the rest of the model to make this easier.

61 Fold the section back up.

62 Reverse the inner section of the point out and squash the layers together.

63 Reverse the inner section of the point out and squash the layers together.

64 Pinch the paper to shape the flowing water.

65 Tuck the point at the top of the flowing water inside the bottle.

66 Complete

Pisces

*

Typically described by two swimming fish, this Pisces model starts from a traditional fish base. The longer points become the tail and the dorsal fin, while the smaller points become the pectoral fins on either side of the body.

18 X 18CM (7 X 7IN)

x1

A

B

C

A 11.75cm   (4½in)
B 7cm   (2¾in)
C 1cm   (½in)

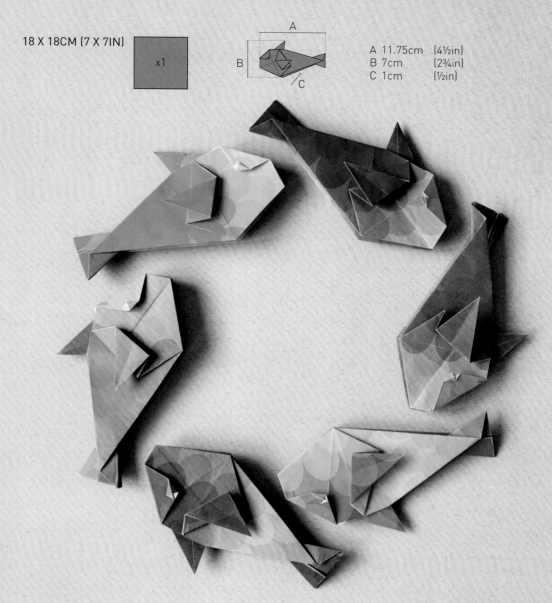

START WITH A SQUARE, COLOURED SIDE UP.

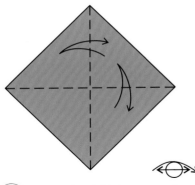

① Fold and unfold the square in half diagonally. Then turn the model over, left to right.

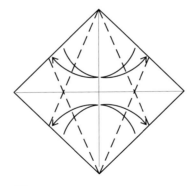

② Fold and unfold the outer edges to the middle crease.

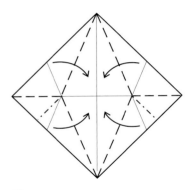

③ Refold the folds from the previous step to make a fish base.

④ Fold out the edges of the upper section to touch the adjacent folded edges, this will open the upper section and make it fold down.

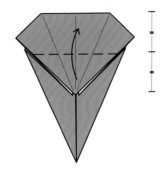

⑤ Fold the corner up to the middle of the folded edge above.

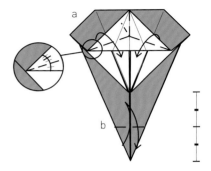

⑥ Fold the sides (a) in and pinch together the upper corner. Then (b) fold and unfold the lower corner.

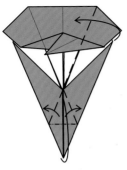

⑦ Fold the edge of the upper section in. Then fold up the lower point and open it up.

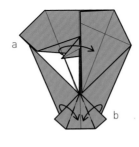

⑧ Fold the corner (a) over. Then fold back the edges (b) of the lower section.

⑨ Fold the left side of the upper section over.

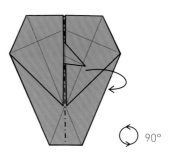

(10) Fold the model in half. Then rotate by 90°.

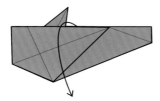

(11) Fold down one side to separate the trapped paper beneath.

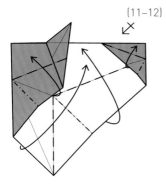

(11–12)

(12) Refold the side back up. Then repeat steps 11 to 12 behind.

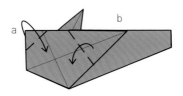

(13) Fold over (a) the outer corner. Then fold over (b) the corner of the middle section.

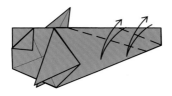

(14) Fold and unfold the rear section twice.

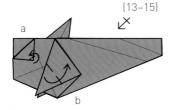

(13–15)

(15) Fold over (a) the tip of the front section to make an eye. Then fold over (b) the corner in the middle to make a fin. Repeat steps 13 to 15 behind.

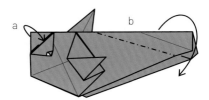

(16) Fold the tip (a) of the head inside the model. Then reverse fold (b) the rear section.

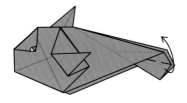

(17) Fold one side of the rear section up to shape the tail.

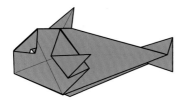

(18) Complete. Make a second to complete the project.

EASTERN ZODIAC

Rat

**

The Eastern or Chinese zodiac cycle typically starts with the Year of the Rat. The model is folded so that the opposing corners of a square become the head and tail of the animal. Add some character to the model by rounding the body and tilting the head.

18 X 18CM (7 X 7IN)

x 1

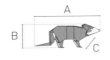

A 12.5cm (5in)
B 4.5cm (1¾in)
C 3cm 1⅓in

START WITH A SQUARE, COLOURED SIDE UP.

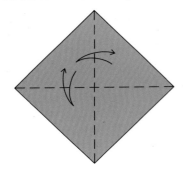

1 Fold and unfold the square diagonally along both axes.

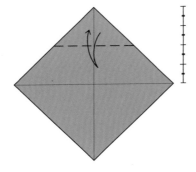

2 Fold and unfold the corner to the middle of the square.

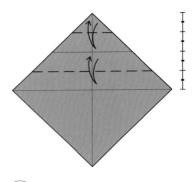

3 Fold and unfold between the creases made previously.

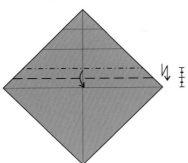

4 Fold the top section down, by folding the crease made previously as a mountain fold, down to the middle line.

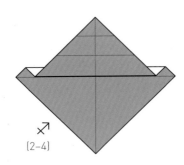

(2–4)

5 Repeat steps 2 to 4 on the lower section.

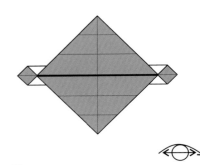

6 Turn the model over, left to right.

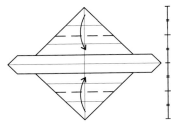 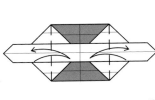 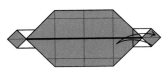 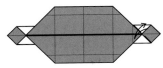

7 Fold the corners to the middle and tuck the corners under the central section.

8 Fold and unfold between the opposite corners. Turn the model over, left to right.

9 Fold and unfold the right side point where indicated.

10 Make a diagonal fold on the point aligned with the edge of the paper. Then unfold.

  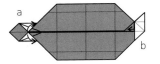 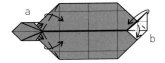

11 Fold the corner over and refold the previous step and open out the paper in the point.

12 Fold the edge back up and flatten the point.

13 On the left side (a), fold the edges out. On the right side (b), fold out the trapped corner beneath.

14 At (a), fold the edges over, this will pull out the adjacent paper. At (b), raise and squash the point.

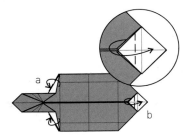 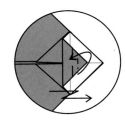 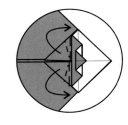 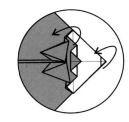

15 At (a), left side: fold the edges over and behind. At (b), right side: fold the upper layer over.

16 Fold the upper layer in and out, making a zigzag fold.

17 Fold the upper layers of the corners over the edge of the head, this will open the ear.

18 Tuck the corners of the ears behind the folded edge and then fold the nose over.

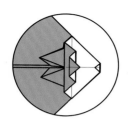

(19) Head complete.

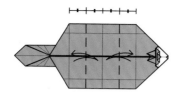

(20) Fold and unfold between the outer creases and the middle fold.

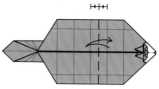

(21) Fold and unfold between the crease made in the previous step and the middle crease.

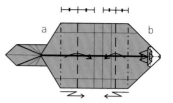

(22) Make two zigzag folds by folding the edges in: (a) should fold to the middle and (b) should fold the edge to the crease made previously.

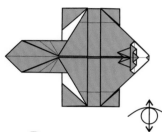

(23) Turn the model over, top to bottom.

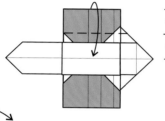

(24) Fold the top edge to the middle.

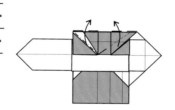

(25) Open the section by folding the upper layer back and leave the lower layer touching the middle section.

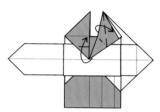

(26) Fold the upper edge of the top layer over and the lower corner back up.

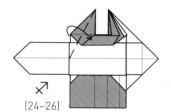

(27) Fold the back corner over between the tip and the middle crease. Repeat steps 24 to 26 on the lower section.

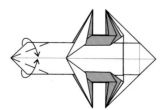

(28) Fold the edges diagonally to touch the middle crease.

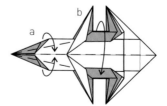

(29) (a) Fold the edges in to the middle again to narrow the tail. (b) Fold the model in half.

(30) Hold the model at the Os. Slide the head down with crimp folds on either side.

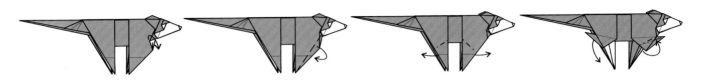

31 Fold the corner of the crimped fold over and fold the upper edge behind the head.

32 Fold the edge of the front section behind and into the model.

33 Reverse fold out the legs by turning them inside out.

34 Reverse fold back the rear leg. Narrow the front leg by folding the edges into the model.

(31–36)

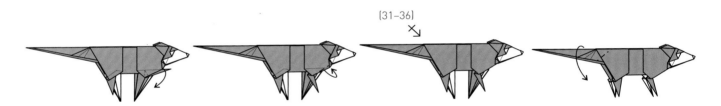

35 Hold the front leg and slide it downwards.

36 Fold the edge of the front section behind.

37 Repeat steps 31 to 36 on the reverse side.

38 Reverse fold the tail by turning it inside out.

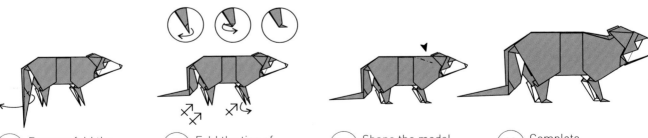

39 Reverse fold the tail again.

40 Fold the tips of the legs back and forward again. Repeat on all legs.

41 Shape the model by folding in a section of the neck.

42 Complete.

Ox

*

The Ox is made in a similar way to Taurus (see page 19), but the proportions of the model are varied to create longer horns and a tail. The character of the model works around the scale of the shoulders, which suggest strength and power.

18 X 18CM (7 X 7IN)

x1

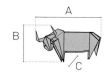

A 9.5cm   (3¾in)
B 5.5cm   (2in)
C 2.25cm (¾in)

START WITH A SQUARE, COLOURED SIDE UP.

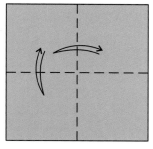

(1) Fold and unfold the square in half lengthwise. Then turn the paper over, left to right.

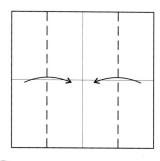

(2) Fold the side edges in to the middle.

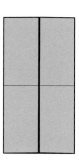

(3) Turn the model over, left to right.

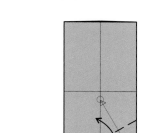

(4) Fold the lower right corner up to the mid-line, starting from the opposite left corner.

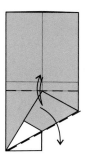

(5) Fold the upper section over the corner and unfold. Then unfold the lower corner.

(6) Fold the lower section up along the crease made in the previous step.

(7) Fold the corner over between the lower corner and the middle of the folded section.

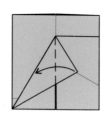

(8) Fold the corner over.

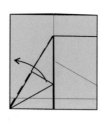

(9) Unfold the folded corner back to step 7.

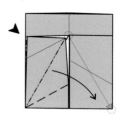

(10) Fold the corner over and open out the point by folding over the upper layer.

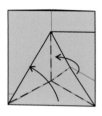

(11) Fold the corner back and fold in the inner section.

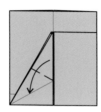

(12) Fold the point down.

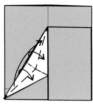

(13) Fold the corner back up. At the same time fold the edge of the middle section in. Repeat steps 7 to 13 on the other side.

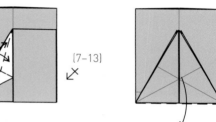

[7–13]

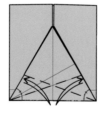

(14) Fold the section down.

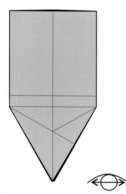

(15) Turn the model over, left to right.

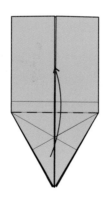

(16) Fold the lower section up again along the crease made previously.

(17) Fold and unfold the triangular section at about one–third of the internal angle.

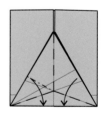

(18) Fold both sides down together along the creases made previously to form a point.

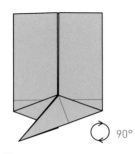

19 Rotate the model by 90°.

$90°$

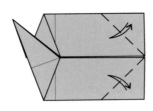

20 Fold and unfold the outer corners.

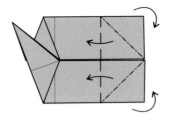

21 Fold the upper layers in while holding the layer beneath. This will cause the outer corners to fold in.

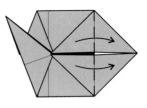

22 Fold the corners back again.

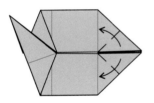

23 Fold the upper layers of the rear section out.

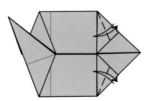

24 Fold and unfold the outer edges in to the vertical folded edges.

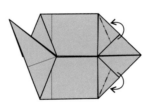

25 Reverse fold the edges inside the folded corners.

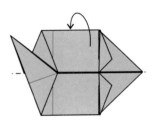

26 Fold the model in half behind.

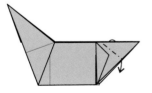

27 Reverse fold the right corner.

28 Reverse fold the two corners inside front and behind to narrow and shape the tail.

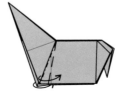

29 Hold the front section and fold it down by making crimp folds in front and behind.

30 Fold the paper beneath the front section up.

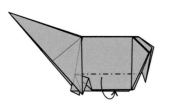

(31) Fold the lower edge into the model.

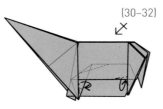

(30–32)

(32) Shape the side by narrowing the front leg and folding a corner of the stomach in. Repeat steps 30 to 32 behind.

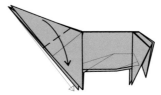

(33) Fold all of the layers of the front point down.

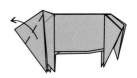

(34) Fold the corner back up again at an angle to shape the head and neck.

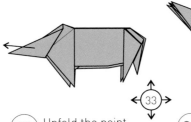

(35) Unfold the point to step 33.

(33)

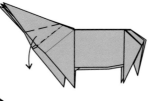

(36) Hold the point and crimp fold it inside the neck along the folds made previously.

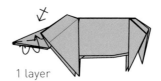

1 layer

(37) Fold one layer of the head up on the front and behind.

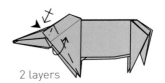

2 layers

(38) Fold over two layers of the front leg and open and squash the upper corner. Repeat behind.

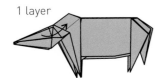

1 layer

(39) Fold over one of the points.

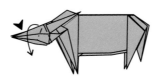

(40) Fold up the front point to be perpendicular to the model. Separate the layers and squash the point flat.

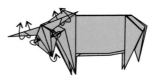

(41) Reverse fold the horns inside out. Then fold in two sides and the tip to shape the head.

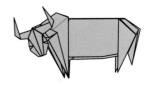

(42) Complete.

Tiger
✳✳✳

The Tiger model works around one of the characteristics of a tiger, its stripes. This model alternates the colours on the front and reverse of the paper to achieve the orange and black effect.

18 X 18CM (7 X 7IN)   x 1

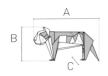

A 10cm (4in)
B 5cm   (2in)
C 3cm   (1⅓in)

START WITH A SQUARE, COLOURED SIDE UP.

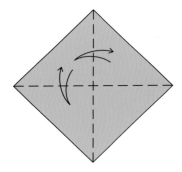

1 Fold and unfold the square diagonally along both axes.

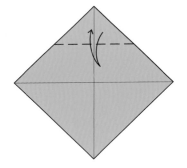

2 Fold and unfold the upper corner to the middle of the square.

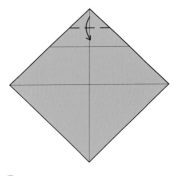

3 Fold the corner in to touch the crease made previously.

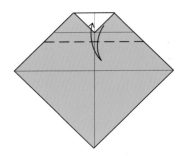

4 Fold and unfold the top edge to the middle line.

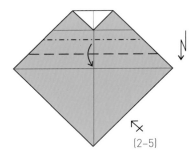

(2–5)

5 Fold the top section down to align the fold made in the previous step to the middle crease. Repeat steps 2 to 5 on the lower section.

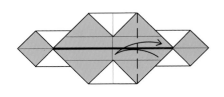

6 Fold and unfold the right side where indicated.

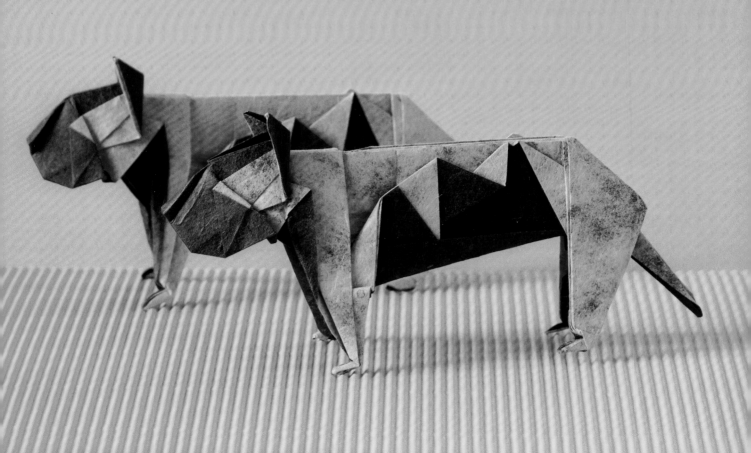

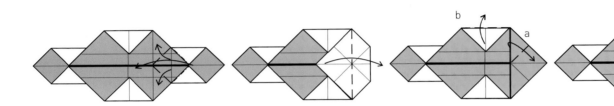

(7) Fold the right section over and open out the adjacent outer point so the inner edges fold out.

(8) Fold the corner back out.

(9) Fold the corner over at (a). Then fold up the upper corner at (b).

(10) Fold the outer edge in diagonally to the middle.

Rear view

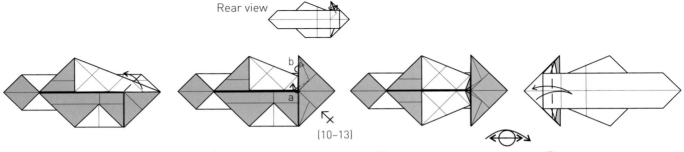

(11) Fold the corner up.

(12) Make a stripe by sliding the paper behind at (b) causing the paper to fold out at (a). Repeat steps 10 to 13 on the other side.

(13) Turn the model over, left to right.

(14) Fold and unfold the left edge to the crease.

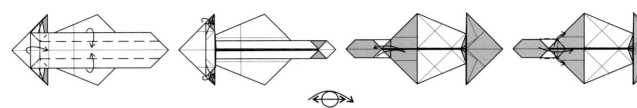

(15) Fold in the outer edges of the middle section and refold the previous step.

(16) Fold the edges of the points in. Then turn the model over, left to right.

(17) Fold and unfold the point where indicated.

(18) Fold the section over along the crease made previously and fold out the sides to open the point.

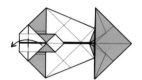

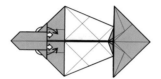

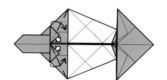

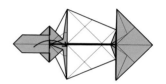

(19) Fold the corner back as shown.

(20) Reverse fold out the paper beneath the front section.

(21) Fold the outer edges of the lower layer in.

(22) Fold the section back over.

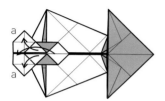

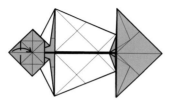

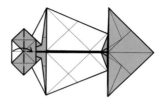

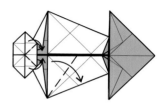

(23) Fold the edges out at (a), causing the section to open out and fold over.

(24) Fold the corner in.

(25) Fold the upper layer of the front section over.

(26) Reverse fold the corners of the front section inside. Then fold the corner in the middle section over to the adjacent edge.

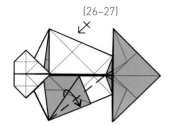

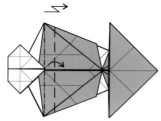

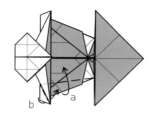

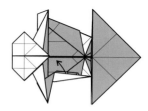

(27) Fold the edge over to the edge again. Repeat steps 26 to 27 on the upper section.

(28) Fold the forward section in and out again, forming a zigzag fold.

(29) Fold the middle section up at (a), causing the point to fold behind at (b).

(30) Slide up the paper folded inside and spread the layers to form stripes.

(29–30)

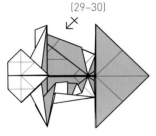 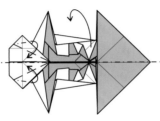 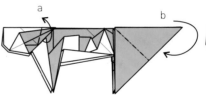 

(31) Repeat steps 29 to 30 on the upper section.

(32) Fold the edges of the front section in and squash them. Fold the model in half behind.

(33) (a) Fold up the ears front and behind. Then (b) reverse fold the rear corner inside the model.

(34) Fold and unfold the edges of the rear section at the front and behind.

  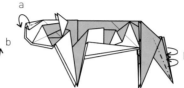 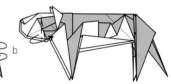

(35) Reverse fold the edges into the model along the creases made previously.

(36) Fold up the corner (a), separate the layers and squash. Then hold the tail at (b) and slide it out.

(37) (a) Fold the edge of the nose behind. Then (b) Fold the edges of the tail inside.

(38) Hold the head and slide it down, making two crimp folds on either side.

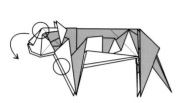  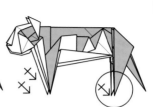  

(39) Hold the head and slide it down slightly.

(40) Fold the edges of the front section behind to narrow and shape the front legs.

(41) Fold the tips of the legs behind and forward again to make the feet.

(42) Complete.

Rabbit

✳✳

The Rabbit starts from a preliminary base. The corners of the square become the front legs, the tail and the head, with the edges evolving into the back legs and the ears. Try adding character and expression to the model by adjusting the angle of the head.

18 X 18CM (7 X 7IN)

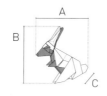

A 6cm (2⅓in)
B 7.5cm (3in)
C 3.5cm (1⅓in)

START WITH A PRELIMINARY BASE WITH THE UPPER CLOSED CORNER REVERSED INSIDE (SINK FOLD). FOLLOW STEPS 1 TO 7 OF AQUARIUS (SEE PAGE 66 TO 68).

1. Reverse fold the corners of the inner section.

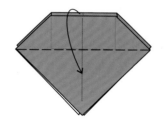

2. Fold down the upper edge to expose the middle of the square.

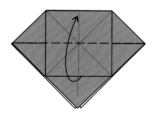

3. Fold the edge back up.

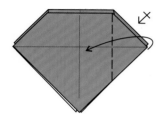

4. Fold the outer corner to the middle front and behind.

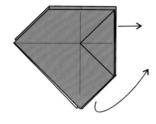

5. Reverse fold out the paper inside the model.

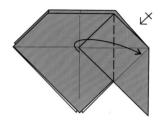

6. Fold the corners back over, front and behind.

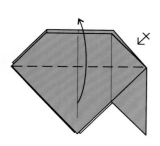

(7) Fold the corners up front and behind.

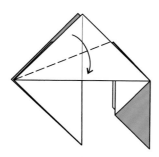

(8) Fold the outer edge down to the adjacent folded edge.

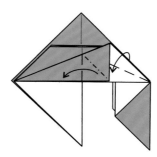

(9) Fold the corner over to the left causing the outer edge to fold over.

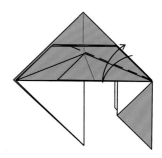

(10) Fold and unfold the inner section over the adjacent crease.

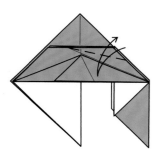

(11) Fold the edge of the inner section to the adjacent crease. Then unfold.

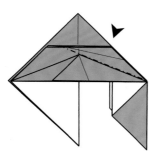

(12) Sink fold the corner inside, along the creases made previously.

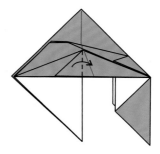

(13) Fold the corner over.

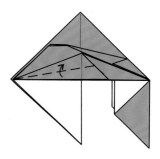

(14) Fold the lower edge up to the adjacent edge. This will open up the paper beneath.

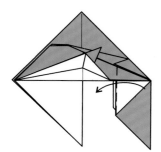

(15) Fold the right corner over as shown.

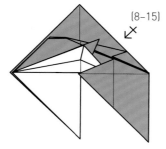

(16) Repeat steps 8 to 15 behind.

(8–15)

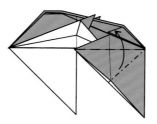

(17) Fold the lower right section up, separate the layers and squash the point flat.

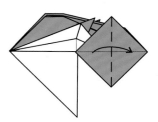

(18) Fold the corner over.

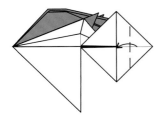

19 Fold the corner over so the tip extends slightly beyond the folded edge beneath.

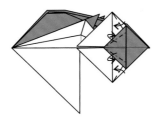

20 Fold the edges of the folded corner behind. This will cause the adjacent edge to fold over too.

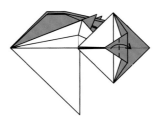

21 Fold the tip over.

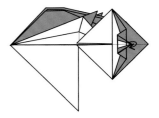

22 Fold the tip behind.

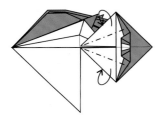

23 Fold the edges of the front section behind.

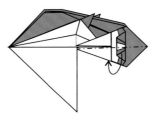

24 Fold the head in half behind.

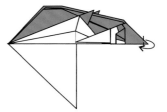

25 Reverse fold the tip over to make a nose. For this, open up the model and refold.

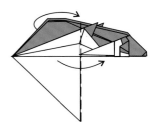

26 Fold the upper layer of the outer corner to the right and open out the folds inside.

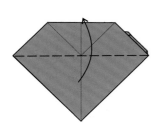

27 Fold the lower corner up.

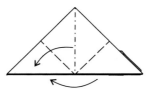

28 Fold the corner back and reverse fold the inner section.

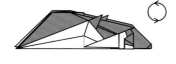

29 Rotate the model.

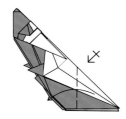

30 Fold the corners over, front and behind.

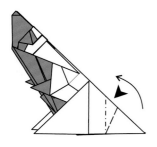

31 Fold the rear section into the model and out again, making a crimp fold.

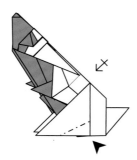

32 Reverse fold the lower corners inside the model, front and behind.

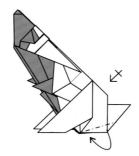

33 Fold the corners into the model, front and behind.

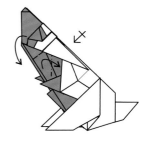

34 Hold the head and slide it down, making two crimp folds on either side to tilt the head.

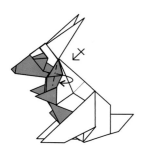

35 Fold the edge of the upper section behind. Repeat on the reverse side.

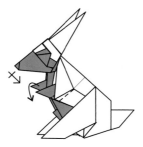

36 Hold the front paws and slide them down slightly, front and behind.

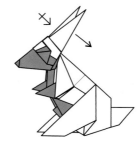

37 Slide the layers apart in the upper point to shape the ears. Tuck the lower edge into the head. Repeat behind.

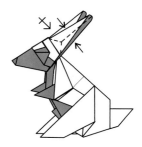

38 Pinch the sides of the ears together. Repeat behind.

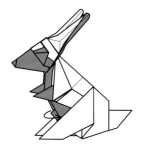

39 Fold the corner into the model.

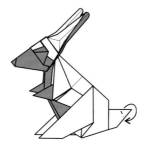

40 Reverse fold the tip of the tail.

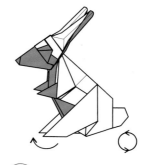

41 Slide the legs forward and rotate slightly to enable the model to balance on its feet.

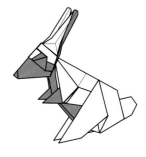

42 Complete.

Dragon
**

The dragon is made from a bird base. The points of the base are folded to become the wings of the dragon. A similar, but more complicated method is used for Scorpio and Cancer.

18 X 18CM (7 X 7IN)

x1

A	11cm (4⅓in)
B	9cm (3½in)
C	7cm (2¾in)

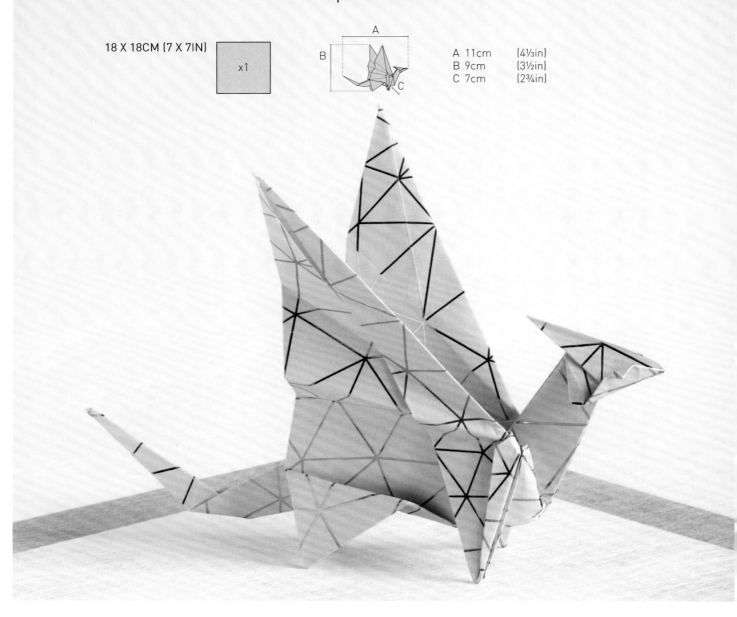

START WITH A SQUARE, COLOURED SIDE UP AND MAKE A BIRD BASE WITH THE UPPER CORNER REVERSED INSIDE (A SINK FOLD). FOLLOW STEPS 1 TO 14 OF CANCER, (SEE PAGES 26 TO 28).

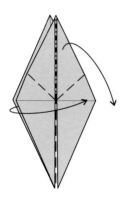

(1) Fold one side over. At the same time reverse fold the point and fold it down to the right.

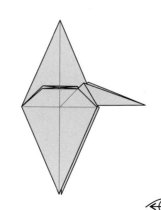

(2) Turn the model over, left to right.

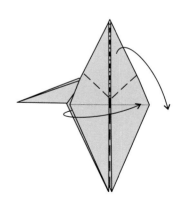

(3) Fold the left edge over and reverse fold the inner section. This fold is higher than the other side.

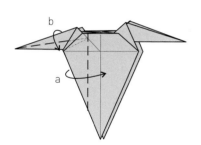

(4) Fold the edge (a) of the middle section over causing (b) the outer edge to fold over.

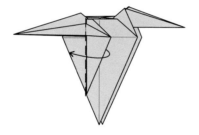

(5) Fold the section back.

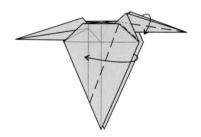

(6) Fold the other edge over, causing the edge of the adjacent point to fold over.

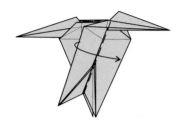

(7) Fold the edge back.

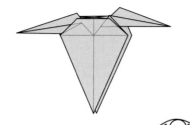

(8) Turn the model over, left to right.

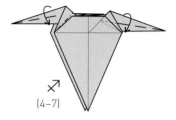

(9) Repeat steps 4 to 7 on the other side.

(4–7)

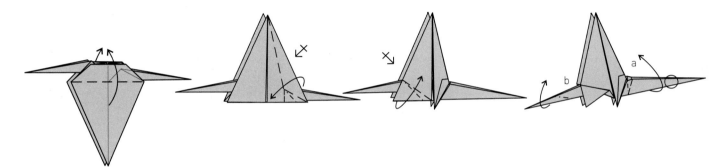

10 Fold the lower points up, front and behind.

11 Fold in the edges of the central triangle, making the lower corner into a point. Repeat behind.

12 Fold the corner up and down again, making a zigzag fold. Repeat behind.

13 Hold point (a) and crimp fold it up. Then reverse fold the point (b) in the middle.

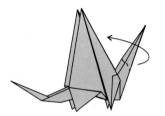

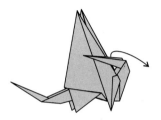

14 Reverse fold the point.

15 Reverse fold the point back again, making a bird's foot fold.

16 Fold out the upper layer. Repeat behind.

17 Reverse fold the tip inside.

18 Fold the edges over front and behind.

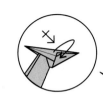

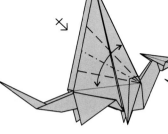

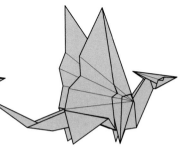

19 Hold the whole head and slide it upwards.

20 Fold the corner up, front and behind.

21 Fold over the tip to make an eye. Repeat behind.

22 Fold and unfold a series of pleats to give the wings texture. Repeat behind.

23 Complete.

Snake

*

The character of the snake comes from the pattern on its body, made from a zigzag fold that interchanges the colours on the front and reverse of the square. The head gives the model personality and brings it to life.

18 X 18CM (7 X 7IN)

x1

A 5.5cm (2in)
B 6cm (2⅓in)
C 27.8cm (11in)

START WITH A SQUARE, COLOURED SIDE UP.

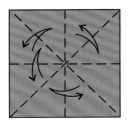

1. Fold and unfold the square in half lengthwise and diagonally along both axes.

2. Fold up the lower right corner. The fold should run from the opposite corner and the middle. Unfold.

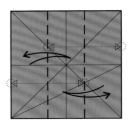

3. Fold the left edge to the intersection of the creases. Then fold the other side over. Then unfold to a square.

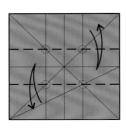

45°

4. Fold and unfold at the intersection of the creases. Then rotate the model by 45° anticlockwise.

5. Fold and unfold a series of four diagonal folds between the points where the creases touch the edges of the square.

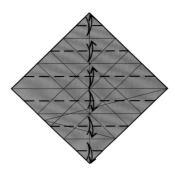

6. Fold and unfold between the creases made previously.

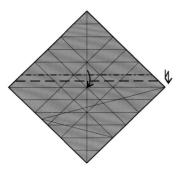

7. Fold the upper section down and up again between the creases.

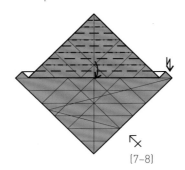

(7–8)

8. Repeat the process making zigzag folds in the upper section. Then repeat steps 7 to 8 on the lower section.

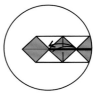

9. Fold the end of the body over behind the first white triangle, then unfold.

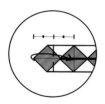

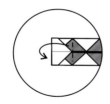

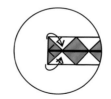

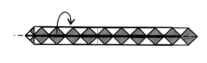

10 Fold the point in to touch the crease made previously.

11 Fold both layers of the point behind.

12 Fold the corners in.

13 Fold the model in half behind.

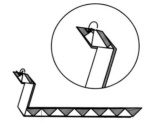

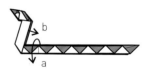

14 Shape the body by turning the front section of the model inside out.

15 Form the head by and turning the upper end of the point inside out.

16 Fold a corner over to make an eye on both sides.

17 (a) Fold some of the lower section of the body down and (b) fold out the paper in the neck.

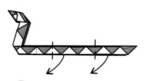

18 Fold the paper back again.

19 Turn the front section inside out to bring the pattern to the front.

20 Fold and shape the body.

21 Complete.

Horse

**

The Horse is simple and elegant in its design, emerging from the folded diagonal axis of the square. Add character to the model by the final shaping of the legs and body, and tilt of the head.

18 X 18CM (7 X 7IN)

x1

A
B
C

A 8.5cm   (3⅓in)
B 7.5cm   (3in)
C 3cm   (1¼in)

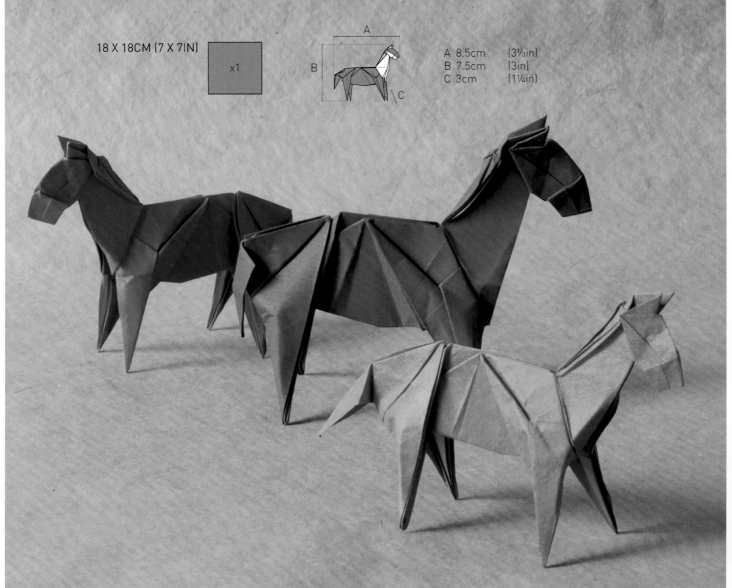

START WITH A SQUARE, COLOURED SIDE UP.

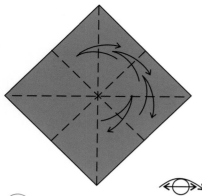

1 Fold and unfold the square in half lengthwise and diagonally along both axes. Then turn the paper over, left to right.

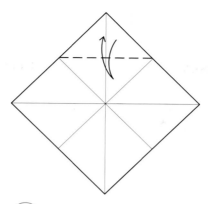

2 Fold the upper corner to the middle of the square, and unfold.

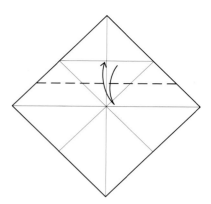

3 Fold and unfold midway between the creases made previously.

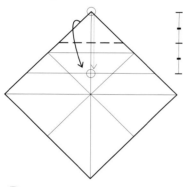

4 Fold the corner down. The point should touch the intersection of the two creases.

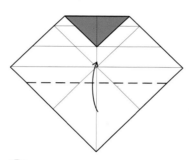

5 Fold the lower corner up to touch the upper folded edge.

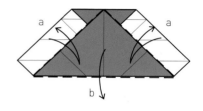

6 Fold and unfold the upper edges (a) along the edges of the folded section. Then fold (b) the corner down again.

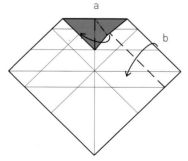

7 Fold the edge of the upper section over at (a) and fold the edge in at (b).

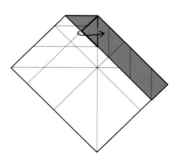

8 Fold the corner back over.

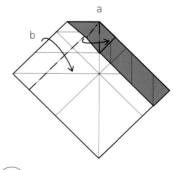

9 Fold the edge (a) over and the side (b) in.

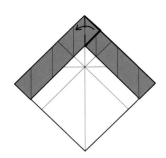

(10) Fold the corner back.

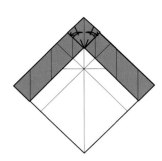

(11) Fold the outer edges of the upper section diagonally in to the middle crease. Then unfold.

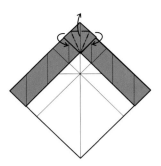

(12) Fold the point up between the creases, causing the edges to fold in.

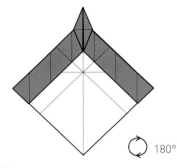

180°

(13) Rotate the model by 180°.

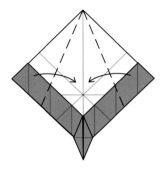

(14) Fold the edges in diagonally to cause the outer edges to touch the middle crease.

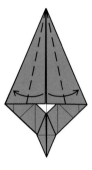

(15) Fold the inner edges out to the adjacent folded edges on both sides.

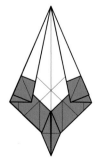

(16) Turn the model over, left to right.

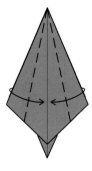

(17) Fold the edges in to the middle.

(18) Fold the upper layer out.

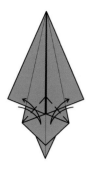

19 Fold and unfold the corners.

20 Fold the lower edges of the upper section up and refold the corners folded previously.

21 Fold the corners down.

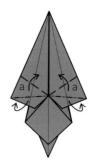

22 Fold the points up at (a) to make the corners touch the creases above. The lower paper will fold in.

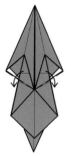

23 Fold the corners back down again.

24 Fold the points back up again and fold the edges of the upper section in.

25 Fold the upper points out, making the inner edges touch the adjacent creases. Fold the lower section up.

26 Fold the lower point down.

27 Fold the upper point down along the upper edge of the folded points.

28 Fold the point back up again. Align the outer right edge of the point with the outer edge of the point behind.

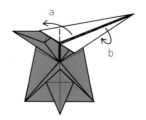

29 Fold the point back to the left at (a), this will cause (b) the lower edge to fold over.

30 Rotate the model 90° clockwise.

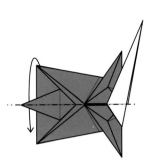

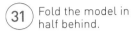

31 Fold the model in half behind.

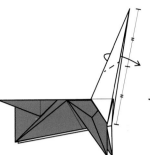

32 Reverse fold the upper point, about half way down, to form the head and neck.

33 Fold down one layer of the reversed point, front and back.

34 Fold the layers around on both sides to turn the point inside out.

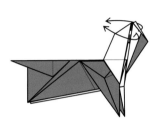

35 Slide the head up by making a Crimp fold on either side of the head. This will form ears.

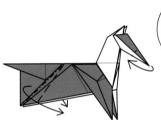

36 Slide the rear section in by making two crimp folds that fold the legs over the body. Fold the tip of the head inside.

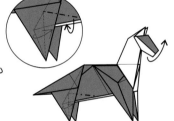

37 Fold in the inner edge of the stomach causing the inner edge of the legs to fold in too. Then slide the head up.

38 (a) Fold the edges of the rear section up. Then (b) Reverse fold the corner inside the model.

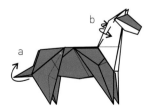

39 (a) Slide the tail up. Then (b) Separate the layers in the neck and fold the edges over.

40 Reverse fold the tail and fold the edge of the hind legs inside. Make a crimp fold to shape the head.

41 Pinch the legs together and shape the front of the model.

42 Complete.

Sheep

**

The Sheep is folded from the lengthwise axis of the square. The legs are simply folded as long extended triangles and the stylized look is completed with a simple head and horns.

18 X 18CM (7 X 7IN)

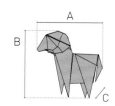

A 6cm   (2⅓in)
B 6.5cm   (2⅓in)
C 3cm   (1¼in)

START BY FOLDING STEPS 1 TO 5 OF TAURUS (SEE PAGE 20).

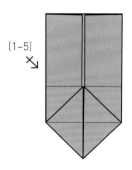

(1–5)

1 Repeat steps 1 to 5 (Taurus, page 20) on the upper section.

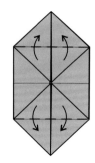

2 Fold the corners out.

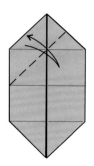

3 Fold and unfold the outer edge.

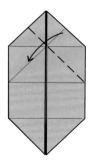

4 Fold the upper edge over.

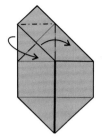

5 Fold the edge back and fold in the opposite side at the same time.

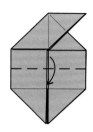

6 Fold the upper section down.

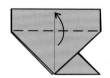

7 Fold the lower section up.

8 Fold the lower corners out to align with the folded edge above.

(9) Fold the model in half behind. Then rotate the model by 90°.

$\circlearrowleft$ 90°

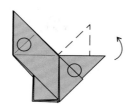

(10) Hold the model where indicated and slide the rear section up.

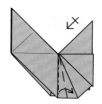

(11) Slide the front section over the rear section with crimp folds on both sides.

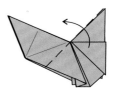

(12) Open the model.

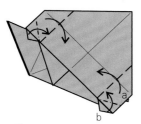

(13) Fold the edge in at (a) to squash (b). Repeat on the upper section.

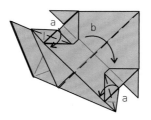

(14) Fold the edges in at (a). Then fold the model in half (b).

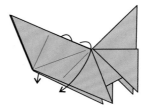

(15) Open out the sides of the front section then turn the upper corner inside out.

Front view.

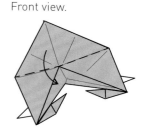

(16) Fold the upper layer of the corner down.

(17) Fold the corner up and down again. Then fold the tip behind.

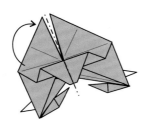

(18) Fold the model back together.

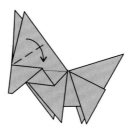

(19) Fold the upper corner over.

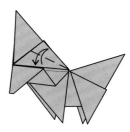

(20) Fold the outer edge diagonally to touch the lower edge. Then unfold.

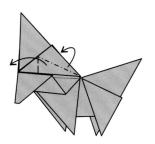

21 Fold the point over and refold the crease made previously to narrow the point.

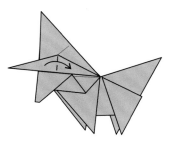

22 Fold the point back again.

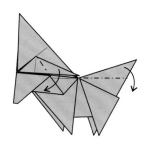

23 Reverse fold the horn, turning it inside out. Then reverse fold the rear point to make a tail.

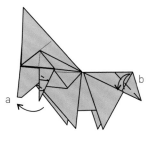

24 (a) Crimp fold and shape the horn. Then (b) fold and unfold the edge of the rear point.

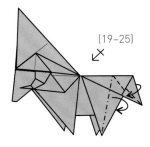

(19–25)

25 Fold the outer edge of the rear legs behind and narrow the tail. Repeat steps 19 to 25 behind.

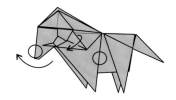

26 Hold the model where indicated and slide the head up..

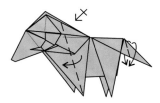

27 Fold the edges in on both sides, tucking the edges beneath the horns. Then turn the rear point inside out.

28 Fold the edge of the head behind on both sides to shape the head.

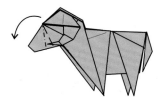

29 Crimp fold the head to shape the face.

30 Crimp fold the body into itself. You will need to open the model to make this fold.

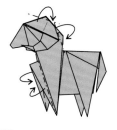

31 Reverse fold the front corner into the model. Then fold the corners behind to shape the horns and neck.

32 Complete.

Monkey

*

The Monkey is described with a few simple folds. The head is formed from a zigzag fold applied to a flattened angular point and the long tail and 'piano-playing' hands enhance the playfulness of the subject.

18 X 18CM (7 X 7IN)

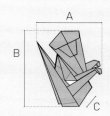

A 8.5cm (3½in)
B 10.5cm (4½in)
C 4cm (1½in)

START WITH A SQUARE, COLOURED SIDE UP.

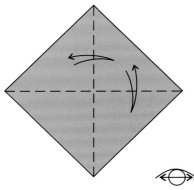

1. Fold and unfold the square diagonally along both axes. Then turn the model over, left to right.

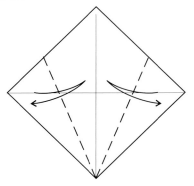

2. Fold the outer edges diagonally to touch the middle crease. Then unfold.

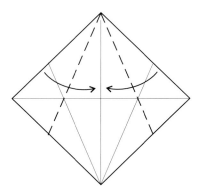

3. Fold the upper edges in diagonally to the middle crease.

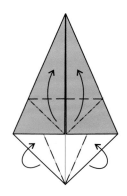

4. Fold the corners up and refold the creases made previously.

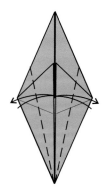

5. Fold and unfold the lower edges in to the middle.

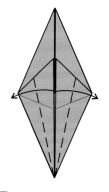

6. Fold the upper layers out to the adjacent folded edges; open up the paper beneath.

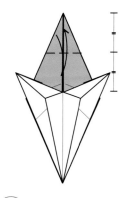

7. Fold the upper corner down to touch the lower fold. Then unfold.

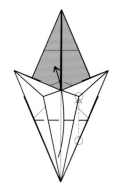

8. Fold the lower point up.

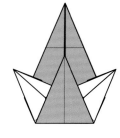

9. Turn the model over, left to right.

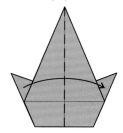

10. Fold the model in half, left to right.

11. Hold the point and slide it out.

12 Fold the upper corner over. The fold should start at the crease made in step 7.

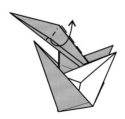

13 Fold the upper layer over, and open and squash the point.

14 Fold the point behind and back out again, making a zigzag fold.

15 Fold the tip of the point behind.

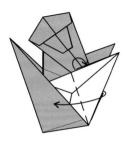

16 Fold the point to the left. This will cause the layer behind to fold over.

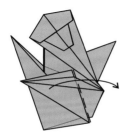

17 Fold the point back again.

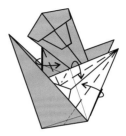

18 Fold the upper and lower edges of the arm in to the middle.

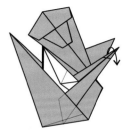

19 Fold over and open the tip, forming the hand.

(16–20)

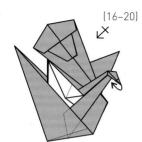

20 Fold the tip of the hand behind. Repeat steps 16 to 20 behind.

21 Fold and unfold the rear section in half.

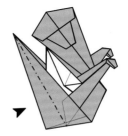

22 Sink fold the outer edge inside to narrow the tail.

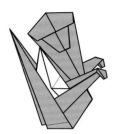

23 Complete.

Rooster

**

The Rooster is made from a stretched bird base. The longer points are folded to make a detailed head and tail. The other corners complete the model by folding into a pair of long, elegant legs in the middle of the model.

18 X 18CM (7 X 7IN)

x1

A 7.5cm   (3in)
B 9.5cm   (3¾in)
C 2cm   (¾in)

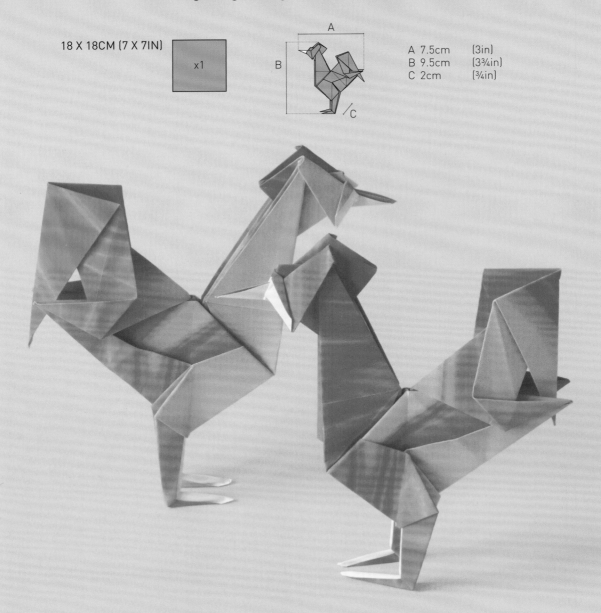

START WITH A SQUARE, COLOURED SIDE UP.

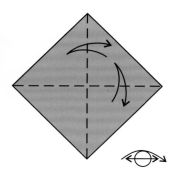

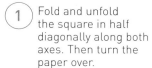

(1) Fold and unfold the square in half diagonally along both axes. Then turn the paper over.

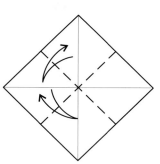

(2) Fold and unfold the square in half lengthwise along both axes.

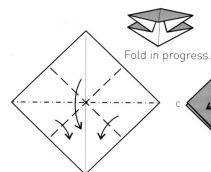

Fold in progress.

(3) Fold the upper half down. At the same time re-fold the creases made previously to make a preliminary base.

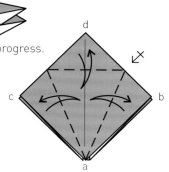

(4) Fold in the edges (a–b) and (a–c) diagonally to the middle. Then fold over the upper triangle. Unfold and repeat behind.

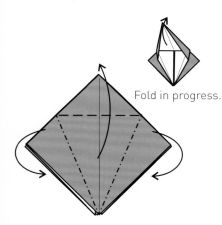

Fold in progress.

(5) Fold the upper layer up along the crease. Fold in the edges. Repeat behind.

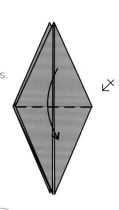

(6) Fold the upper corner down. repeat behind.

(7) Open up the model back to a square.

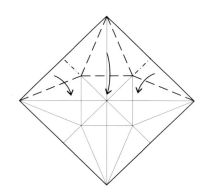

(8) Fold the upper section down along the creases made previously.

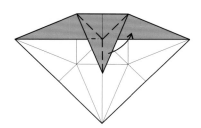

(9) Pinch the ends of the point together. Fold it to the right.

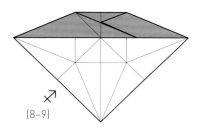

(8–9)

(10) Repeat steps 8 to 9 on the lower section.

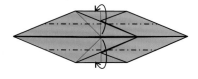

(11) Fold the edges behind to touch the middle crease.

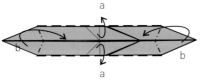

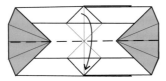

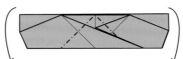

12 Fold out the upper layers at (a). This will cause the outer corners to fold in at (b).

13 Fold the model in half.

14 Reverse fold the outer corners inside the model.

15 Fold one side over to expose the inner face.

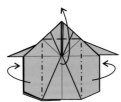

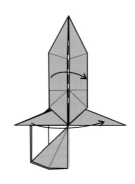

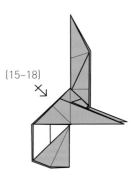

(15–18)

16 Fold the upper layer up. This will cause the outer edges to fold in.

17 Reverse out the paper trapped in the upper section.

18 Fold the left side of the upper section over.

19 Repeat steps 15 to 18 on the other side.

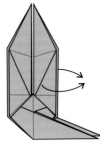

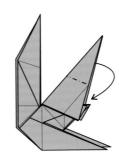

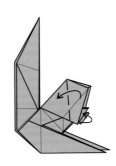

20 Fold out the trapped paper, reversing the corners front and behind.

21 Hold the point and slide it down, making two crimp folds front and behind.

22 Reverse fold the corner inside.

23 Fold the edge over at the front and behind. This will cause the paper beneath to fold over.

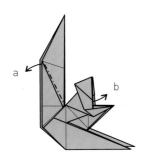

24 (a) Reverse fold the front section. (b) Then fold out the paper trapped in the rear section.

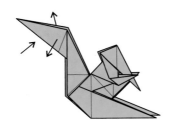

25 Separate the layers of the front section and open out the paper inside.

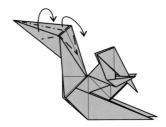

26 Fold out the paper in the opened point and squash the head, reversing out the paper.

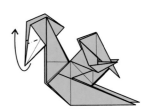

27 Reverse fold the corner up again.

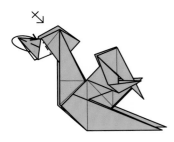

28 Fold the sides up and into the head at the front and behind.

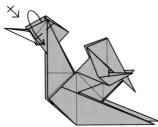

29 Fold the edges of the head over front and behind.

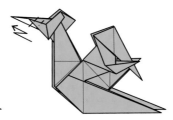

30 Fold the corner point in and out, making a zigzag fold.

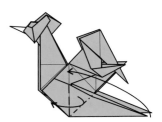

31 Fold the lower corner up, seperate the layers and squash the point flat.

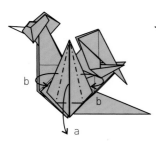

32 Fold the point down at (a) and fold the edges in at (b), narrowing the point.

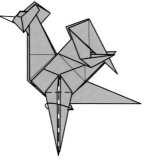

33 Fold the point in half.

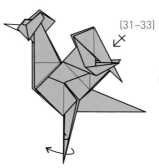

34 Repeat steps 31 to 33 behind. Then folds in the tips of both legs with bird's-foot folds to make feet.

35 Complete. Make the model stand by changing the angle of the feet.

Dog
**

The Dog is another stylized model with features described by simple folds. The character of the model is emphasized by the angle of the back, the tilt of the head and the angle of the tail. Try experimenting with natural textured paper to bring the model to life.

18 X 18CM (7 X 7IN)

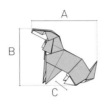

A 8.6cm   (3⅓in)
B 8.6cm   (3⅓in)
C 3cm   (1in)

START WITH A SQUARE, COLOURED SIDE UP.

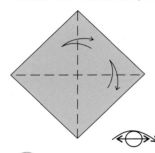

1) Fold and unfold the square in half diagonally along both axes. Then turn the paper over, left to right.

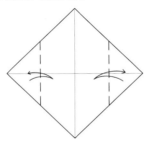

2) Fold the corners to the middle of the square. Then unfold.

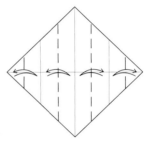

3) Fold and unfold midway between the creases made previously.

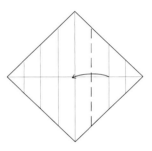

4) Fold one side in along the crease made previously.

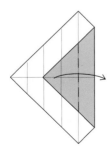

5) Fold the section back along the adjacent crease.

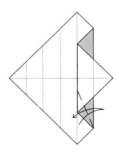

6) Fold the edge of the lower corner to touch the outer edge. Then unfold.

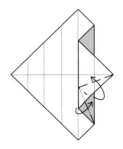

7) Fold the edge of the middle section up. This will cause the lower edge to fold up.

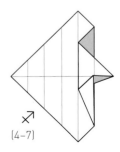

(4–7)

8) Repeat steps 4 to 7 on the other side.

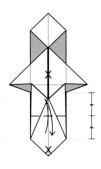
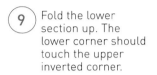

(9) Fold the lower section up. The lower corner should touch the upper inverted corner.

(10) Fold the lower section up and open up the sides of the lower section.

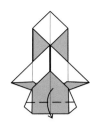

(11) Fold the point back down again.

(12) Fold the sides of the lower section in diagonally to the mid-line. This will cause the adjacent edges to fold in.

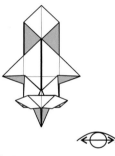

(13) Turn the model over, left to right.

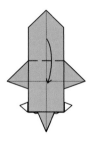

(14) Fold the upper section down.

(15) Fold and unfold along the edges.

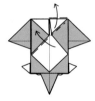

(16) Fold the section up along the diagonal crease and open up one side.

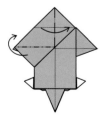

(17) Fold the side over.

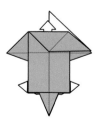

(18) Fold out the trapped paper.

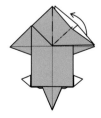

(19) Fold up the section, separate the layers and squash flat.

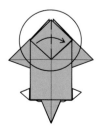

(20) Fold one side over.

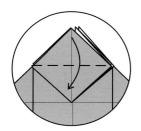

(21) Fold the upper layer only down.

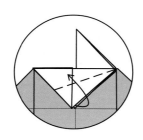

(22) Fold the edge up to the adjacent folded edge.

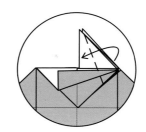

(23) Fold the upper layer of the edge in.

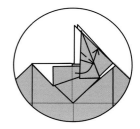

(24) Slide the lower section up to make two diagonal folds.

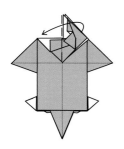

(25) Fold over the upper section.

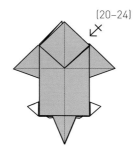

(20–24)

(26) Repeat steps 20 to 24 on the other side.

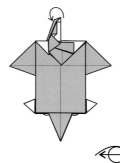

(27) Reverse fold the tip into the head. Then turn the model over, left to right.

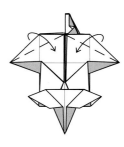

(28) Fold the upper corners down.

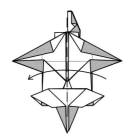

(29) Fold the model in half.

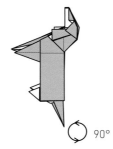

90°

(30) Rotate the model by 90° anticlockwise.

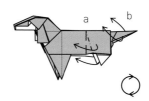

(31) (a) Crimp the hind legs over the body. (b) Then turn the tail inside out.

(32) Complete.

Pig
**

The Pig completes the cycle of the eastern zodiac. The final model allows for some sculpting to give volume to the body. You can also add character to the model by tilting the ears and the tail.

18 X 18CM (7 X 7IN)   x 1

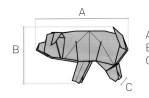

A 8cm   (3in)
B 5.5cm   (2in)
C 3.5cm   (1⅓in)

START WITH A PRELIMINARY BASE WITH THE UPPER CLOSED CORNER REVERSED INSIDE (SINK FOLD). START FROM STEP 7 OF AQUARIUS (SEE PAGE 66 TO 68).

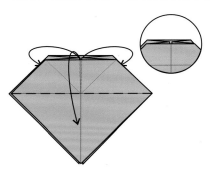

(1) Fold down the upper edge and open out the middle section.

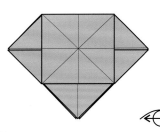

(2) Turn the model over, left to right.

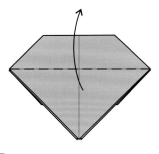

(3) Fold the lower corner up.

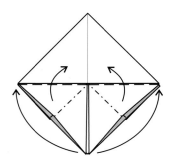

(4) Fold the corners up, separate the layers and squash flat.

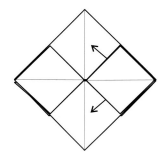

(5) Fold out the trapped paper.

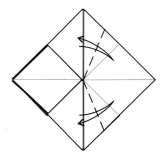

(6) Fold the edges diagonally to the adjacent creases. Unfold.

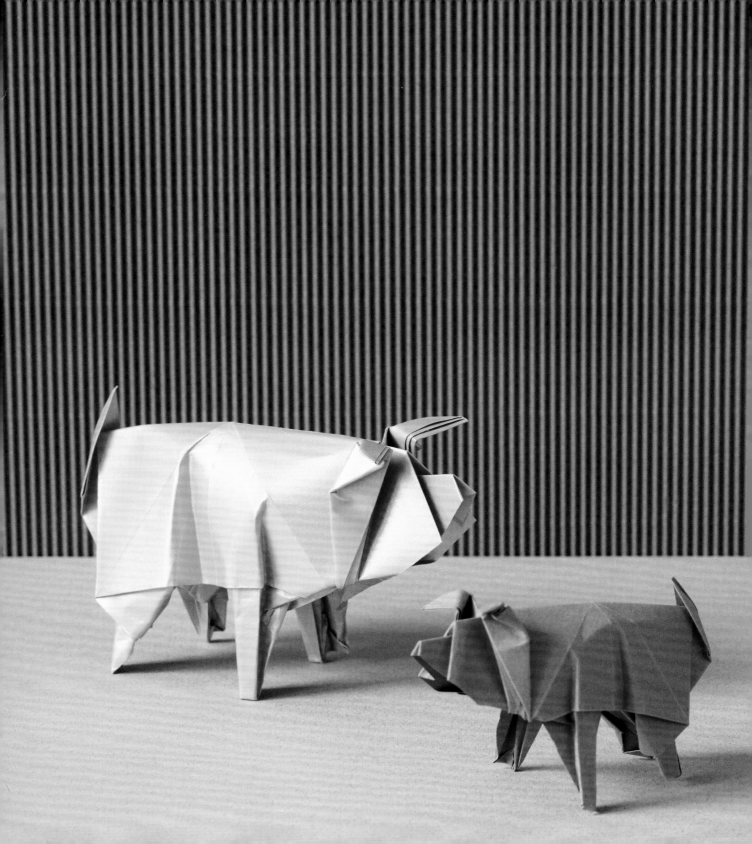

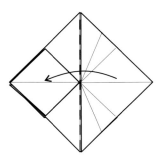

(7) Fold one side over.

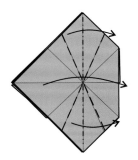

(8) Fold the corner back and reverse fold the corners inside along the creases made previously.

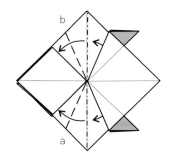

(9) Fold the corners (a) and (b) to the front, pulling out the paper behind the rear section.

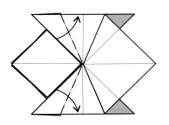

(10) Fold the corners back over.

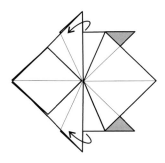

(11) Fold the paper in the lower layer to the front.

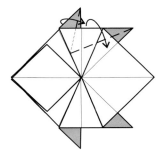

(12) Fold the edge over, this will cause the paper above to fold over.

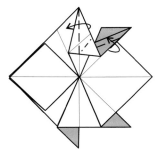

(13) Fold the edge of the upper section over and fold over the adjacent edge.

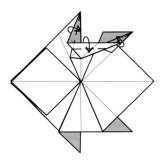

(14) Fold the edge down. This will cause the edges of the adjacent paper to fold in.

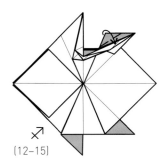

(15) Fold the corner over. Then repeat steps 12 to 15 on the lower section.

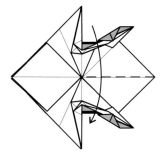

(16) Fold the model in half.

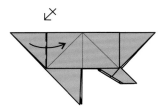

(17) Fold one corner over. Repeat behind.

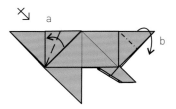

(18) (a) Fold the corner over front and behind. Then (b) reverse fold the back section into the model.

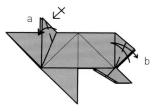

(19) (a) Fold the edge of the front triangles over. Then (b) fold and unfold the edge of the rear section. Repeat behind.

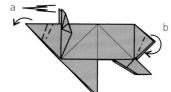

(20) (a) fold the front corner in and out again. Then (b) reverse fold the edges in along the creases made previously.

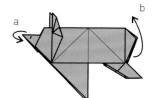

(21) (a) Reverse fold the tip. Then (b) fold the tail up.

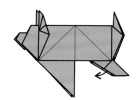

(22) Fold out the inner layer of the rear leg.

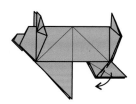

(23) Make a crimp fold to slide the lower point of the leg forwards.

(22–24)

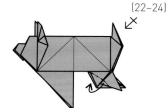

(24) Fold the edge behind to lock the crimp fold made previously. Then repeat steps 22 to 24 behind.

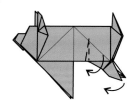

(25) Hold the rear section and slide it down by making two crimp folds on either side, to shape the body.

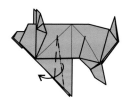

(26) Crimp the legs on both sides and slide the edges over the forward section.

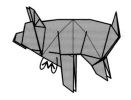

(27) Fold the edges in to narrow the neck. Repeat behind.

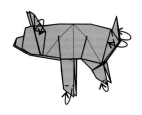

(28) Fold the ears down, and shape the feet. Repeat behind. Then turn the tail inside out.

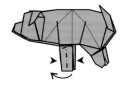

(29) Pinch the front feet together and shape the legs to balance the model and make it stand.

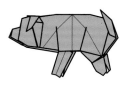

(30) Complete.

RESOURCES AND ACKNOWLEDGEMENTS

AUTHOR'S WEBSITE
Creaselightning
www.creaselightning.co.uk
Mark Bolitho's website featuring
his work.

ORIGAMI SOCIETIES
Asociación Española de
Papiroflexia (Spain)
www.pajarita.org
Spanish origami society.

British Origami Society (UK)
www.britishorigami.info
One of the oldest and most
established origami societies.

CDO (Italy)
www.origami-cdo.it
Italian origami society

Japan Origami Academic Society
– JOAS (Japan)
Origami.gr.jp
Japanese origami association
with a good magazine on
advanced folding techniques.

MFPP (France)
www.mfpp-origami.fr
French origami society

Nippon Origami Association
(Japan)
www.origami-noa.jp
Japanese origami society

Origami Australia
origami.org.au
Australian origami society

Origami Deutschland
www.papierfalten.de
German origami society

Origami USA
www.origamiusa.org
With headquarters in New York,
this society holds one of the
biggest origami conventions
of the year.

OTHER ORGANIZATIONS
Colour Tree Ltd (UK)
www.colortreelimited.co.uk
Good supplies of origami papers.

European Origami Museum
(Spain)
www.emoz.es
An origami museum in
Zaragoza, Spain.

John Gerard Paper studios
(Germany)
www.gerard-paperworks.com
Paper maker with a range of
handmade papers.

Origami Spirit (USA)
www.origamispirit.com
Origami blog and a range of
interesting projects.

Origamido Studios (USA)
www.origamido.com
A paper art studio that also
produces bespoke paper for
origami artists.

Shepherds Falkiners Fine Paper
(UK)
store.bookbinding.co.uk
UK-based supplier of fine papers.

AUTHOR'S ACKNOWLEDGEMENTS
Thanks to Marion, John, Rie, Simon, Beth, Luke, Alex, Talia, Nick, Jen, Annabelle, Jack, Ollie and Graham,
and to my friends and family for their support in my origami journey.